Thanks for the

E-mails

Compiled by Stuart Kira

Enjoy

[signature] x

KP

KIRA PUBLISHING

Published in the United Kingdom in 2010 by Kira Publishing
Hatfield, Herts, UK

ISBN: 978-0-9566644-0-2

CONTENTS

Love and Marriage ...

Husband of the year awards!

The honourable mention goes to:

The United Kingdom

4

Love and Marriage ...

...followed closely by

The United States of America

and then...

Love and Marriage ...

Poland

Love and Marriage ...

but 3rd Place must go to

Greece

it was very very close
but the runner up prize
was awarded to ...

7

Love and Marriage ...

Serbia

but the winner of the
husband/partner of the year is ...

Love and Marriage ...

Ireland

Ya gotta love the Irish.

The Irish are true romantics,
Look, he's even holding her hand.

Love and Marriage ...

Loving Wife

A man breaks into a house to look for money and guns. Inside, he finds a couple in bed. He orders the guy out of the bed and ties him to a chair. While tying the homeowner's wife to the bed the convict gets on top of her, kisses her neck, then gets up and goes into the bathroom.

While he's in there, the husband whispers over to his wife:

'Listen, this guy is an escaped convict. Look at his clothes! He's probably spent a lot of time in jail and hasn't seen a woman in years. I saw how he kissed your neck. If he wants sex, don't resist, don't complain ... do what ever he tells you. Satisfy him no matter how much he nauseates you. This guy is obviously very dangerous. If he gets angry, he'll kill us both. Be strong, honey. I love you!'

His wife responds:

'He wasn't kissing my neck. He was whispering in my ear. He told me that he's gay, thinks you're cute, and asked if we had any Vaseline. I told him it was in the bathroom. Be strong honey. I love you too.'

Love and Marriage ...

The husband had just finished reading a new book entitled:

'YOU CAN BE THE MAN
OF YOUR HOUSE'

He stormed to his wife in the kitchen and announced:

'From now on, you need to know that I am the man of this house, and my word is Law. You will prepare me a gourmet meal tonight; and when I'm finished eating my meal, you will serve me a sumptuous dessert.

After dinner, you are going to go upstairs with me and we will have the kind of pleasure that I want.

Afterwards, you are going to pour a bath for me so I can relax. You will wash my back and towel me dry and bring me my robe. Then, you will massage my feet and hands.

Then tomorrow, guess who's going to dress?'

The wife replied:

'The fu**ing funeral director would be my first guess!'

Love and Marriage ...

Jacqueline and her husband Marc went for counselling after 25 years of marriage...

When asked what the problem was, Jacqueline went into a passionate, painful tirade listing every problem they had ever had in the 25 years they had been married.

She went on and on and on: neglect, lack of intimacy, emptiness, loneliness, feeling unloved and unlovable, an entire laundry list of unmet needs she had endured over the course of their marriage.

Finally, after allowing this to go on for a sufficient length of time, the therapist got up, walked around the desk and, after asking Jacqueline to stand, unbuttoned her blouse, embraced her, put his hands on her breasts, and kissed her passionately as her husband Marc watched with a raised eyebrow.

Jacqueline shut up, buttoned up her blouse, and quietly sat down as though in a daze.

The therapist turned to Marc and said :
'This is what your wife needs at least three times a week.
Can you do this?'

Marc thought for a moment and replied:
'Well, I can drop her here on Mondays and Wednesdays,
but on Fridays I play golf'

Love and Marriage ...

Voted Best Joke in New Zealand

Bruce walks into his bedroom with a sheep under his arm and says:

'Darling, this is the pig I have sex with when you have a headache.'

His wife is lying in bed and replies:

'I think you'll find that's a sheep, you idiot.'

Bruce says:
'I think you'll find that I wasn't talking to you.

BALLS AND GUTS

– THOUGHT YOU MIGHT WANT TO KNOW THE DIFFERENCE

Medical Distinction

We've all heard about people having guts or balls. But do you really know the difference between them? In an effort to keep you informed:

GUTS

- is arriving home late after a night out with the guys, being met by your wife with a broom, and having the guts to ask, 'Are you still cleaning, or are you flying somewhere?'

BALLS

- is coming home late after a night out with the guys, smelling of perfume and beer, lipstick on your collar, slapping your wife on the butt and having the balls to say, 'You're next.'

I hope this clears up any confusion.

Medically speaking, there is no difference in the outcome, since both ultimately result in death.

Love and Marriage ...

A couple was on their honeymoon, lying in bed, ready to consummate their marriage, when the new bride says to the husband, 'I have a confession to make, I'm not a virgin.'
The husband replies, 'That's no big thing in this day and age.'
The wife continues, 'Yeah, I've been with one guy.'
'Oh yeah? Who was the guy?'
'Tiger Woods.'
'Tiger Woods the golfer?'
'Yeah.'
'Well he's rich, famous and handsome. I can see why you went to bed with him.'

The husband and wife then make passionate love. When they finish, the husband gets up and walks to the telephone.

'What are you doing?' asks his wife.
The husband says, 'I'm hungry, I was going to call room service and get some food.'
'Tiger wouldn't do that!' she claims.
'Oh yeah? What would Tiger do?'
'He'd come back to bed and do it a second time.'

The husband puts down the phone and goes back to bed to make love with his wife a second time. When they finish, he gets up and goes over to the phone ...

Love and Marriage ...

'What are you doing?' she asks.
The husband says, 'I'm still hungry so I was going to call room service to get some food.'
'Tiger wouldn't do that,' again she claims.
'Oh yeah? What would Tiger do?'
'He'd come back to bed and do it a third time.'

The guy slams down the phone and goes back to bed and makes love to his wife a third time. When they finish hes tired and beat. He drags himself over to the phone and starts to dial.

The wife asks,
'Are you calling room service?'

'No! I'm calling Tiger Woods to find out what's par for this damn hole!'

Love and Marriage ...

A married man left work early one Friday, but instead of going home, he spent the weekend partying with the boys.

When he finally returned home on Sunday night, his wife really got on his case and stayed on it.

After a few of hours of swearing and screaming, his wife paused and pointed at him and made him an offer. 'How would you like it if you didn't see me for a couple of days?'

The husband couldn't believe his luck, so he looked up, smiled and said, 'That would suit me just fine!!'

Monday went by, and the man didn't see his wife.
Tuesday and Wednesday went by and he still didn't see her.

Come Thursday, the swelling went down a bit and he could see her a little out of the corner of his left eye.

Love and Marriage ...

A man and his ever-nagging wife went on vacation to Jerusalem. While they were there, the wife passed away.

The undertaker told the husband 'You can have her shipped home for $5,000 or you can bury her here, in the Holy Land for $150'

The husband thought about it and told him he would just have her shipped home. The undertaker asked 'Why would you spend $5,000 to ship your wife home, when it would e wonderful to be buried here and you would only spend $150?'

The man replied 'Long ago, a man died here, was buried here and three days later he rose from the dead. I just cannot take that chance'

Love and Marriage ...

My wife sat down on the couch next to me as I was flipping channels.
She asked, 'What's on TV?'
I said, 'Dust.'
And then the fight started ...

My wife was hinting about what she wanted for our upcoming anniversary. She said, 'I want something shiny that goes from 0 to 100 in about 3 seconds.'
I bought her a set of bathroom scales.
And then the fight started ...

When I got home last night, my wife demanded that I take her someplace expensive ... so, I took her to a gas station.
And then the fight started ...

My wife and I were sitting at a table at my high school reunion, and I kept staring at a drunken lady swigging her drink as she sat alone at a nearby table.
My wife asked, 'Do you know her?'
'Yes,' I sighed, 'She's my old girlfriend. I understand she took to drinking right after we split up those many years ago, and I hear she hasn't been sober since.'
'My God!' says my wife, 'who would think a person could go on celebrating that long?'
And then the fight started ...

Love and Marriage ...

After retiring, I went to the Social Security office to apply for Social Security.
The woman behind the counter asked me for my driver's license to verify my age. I looked in my pockets and realized I had left my wallet at home.
I told the woman that I was very sorry, but I would have to go home and come back later.
The woman said, 'Unbutton your shirt'.
So I opened my shirt revealing my curly silver hair.
She said, 'That silver hair on your chest is proof enough for me' and she processed my Social Security application.
When I got home, I excitedly told my wife about my experience at the Social Security office.
She said, 'You should have dropped your pants. You might have gotten disability, too.'
And then the fight started ...

I took my wife to a restaurant.
The waiter, for some reason, took my order first.
'I'll have the strip steak, medium rare, please.'
He said, 'Aren't you worried about the mad cow?'
'Nah, she can order for herself.'
And then the fight started...

My wife asked me if a certain dress made her butt look big.
I told her not as much as the dress she wore yesterday and then the fight started ...

Love and Marriage ...

A woman is standing nude, looking in the bedroom mirror.
She is not happy with what she sees and says to her husband,
'I feel horrible; I look old, fat and ugly. I really need you to pay me
a compliment.'
The husband replies, 'Your eyesight's damn near perfect.'
And then the fight started ...

I tried to talk my wife into buying a case of Miller Light for
16.99 euros. Instead, she bought a jar of cold cream for 7.99
euros. I told her the beer would make her look better at
night than the cold cream.
And then the fight started ...

A man and a woman were asleep like two innocent babies.

Suddenly, at 3 o'clock in the morning, a loud noise came from
outside. The woman, bewildered, jumped up from the bed and
yelled at the man 'Holy crap. That must be my husband!'

So the man jumped out of the bed; scared and naked jumped
out the window. He smashed himself on the ground, ran
through a thorn bush and to his car as fast as he could go.

A few minutes later he returned and went up to the bedroom
and screamed at the woman, 'I AM your husband!'
The woman yelled back, 'Yeah, then why were you running?'
And then the fight started ...

Love and Marriage ...

Saturday morning I got up early, quietly dressed, made my lunch, grabbed the dog, and slipped quietly into the garage. I hooked up the boat up to the truck, and proceeded to back out into a torrential downpour. The wind was blowing 50 mph, so I pulled back into the garage, turned on the radio, and discovered that the weather would be bad all day. I went back into the house, quietly undressed, and slipped back into bed. I cuddled up to my wife's back, now with a different anticipation, and whispered, 'The weather out there is terrible.'
My loving wife of 10 years replied,
'Can you believe my stupid husband is out fishing in that?'
And then the fight started . . .

I asked my wife, 'Where do you want to go for our anniversary?'
It warmed my heart to see her face melt in sweet appreciation. 'Somewhere I haven't been in a long time!' she said.
So I suggested, 'How about the kitchen?'
And that's when the fight started ...

My wife and I are watching 'Who Wants To Be A Millionaire' while we were in bed.
I turned to her and said, 'Do you want to have sex?'
'No,' she answered.
I then said, 'Is that your final answer?'
She didn't even look at me this time, simply saying 'Yes.'
So I said, 'Then I'd like to phone a friend.'
And that's when the fight started ...

Love and Marriage ...

Imagine the following:

You have just made it through your wedding ceremony and have stepped out on the front steps of the church.

The photographer raises his camera. Following a family tradition, both of you hold white doves which you will release together.

You and your new bride stand shoulder to shoulder with a dove in your hands as your friends and family eagerly wait. The photographer gives the signal and you and your bride open your hands toward the sky ...

Love and Marriage ...

Not a dry eye anywhere,
the camera flashes ...

the moment is saved for eternity.

You thought the doves were going to poop,
didn't you?

A man was leaving a cafe with his morning coffee when he noticed a most unusual funeral procession approaching the nearby cemetery. A long black hearse was followed by a second long black hearse about 50 feet behind the first.

Behind the second hearse was a solitary man walking a pit-bull on a leash.

Behind him was a queue of 200 men walking in single file.

The man couldn't stand the curiosity. He respectfully approached the man walking the dog. 'I am so sorry for your loss, and I know now is a bad time to disturb you, but I've never seen a funeral like this with so many of you walking in single file. Whose funeral is it?'

The man replied, 'Well, the first hearse is for my wife'
'What happened to her?'

The man replied 'My dog attacked and killed her.'

He inquired further, 'Well, who is in the second hearse?'
The man answered, 'My Mother-in-law. She was trying to help my wife when the dog turned on her.'

A poignant and thoughtful moment of silence passes between the two men.
'Can I borrow the dog?'
'Yes, join the queue'

Love and Marriage ...

choosing a wife

A man wanted to get married. He was having trouble choosing among three likely candidates. He gives each woman a present of £5,000 and watches to see what they do with the money.

The first does a total makeover. She goes to a fancy beauty salon, gets her hair done, new make up and buys several new outfits and dresses up very nicely for the man.
She tells him that she has done this to be more attractive for him because she loves him so much.
The man was impressed.

The second goes shopping to buy the man gifts. She gets him a new set of golf clubs, some new gizmos for his computer, and some expensive clothes. As she presents these gifts, she tells him that she has spent all the money on him because she loves him so much.
Again, he man is impressed.

The third invests the money in the stock market. She earns several times the £5,000. She gives him back his £5,000 and reinvests the remainder in a joint account. She tells him that she wants to save for their future because she loves him so much.
Obviously, the man was very impressed.

The man thought for a long time about what each woman had done with the money he'd given her, and then made his decision

He married the one with the biggest boobs !!!

Love and Marriage ...

MENS' CONSIDERATIONFOR WOMEN

It is important for men to remember that, as women grow older, it becomes harder for them to maintain the same quality of housekeeping as when they were younger.

When you notice this, try not to yell at them. Some are oversensitive, and there's nothing worse than an oversensitive woman.

My name is Kevin. Let me relate how I handled the situation with my wife.

Since I retired several years ago, it has become necessary for her to get a full-time job along with her part-time job, both for extra income and for the health insurance benefits that we needed.

Shortly after she started working, I noticed she was beginning to show her age. I usually get home from the golf club about the same time she gets home from work. Although she knows how hungry I am, she almost always says she has to rest for half an hour or so before she starts dinner. I don't yell at her. Instead, I tell her to take her time and just wake me when she gets dinner on the table. I generally have lunch in the Men's Grill at the club so eating out is costly and not reasonable and I'm ready for some home-cooked grub when I hit that door.

Love and Marriage ...

She used to do the dishes as soon as we finished eating. But now it's not unusual for them to sit on the table for several hours after dinner. I do what I can by diplomatically reminding her several times each evening that they won't clean themselves. I know she really appreciates this, as it does seem to motivate her to get them done before she goes to bed.

Another symptom of aging is complaining, I think. For example she will say that it is difficult for her to find time to pay the monthly bills during her lunch hour. But, boys, we take 'em for better or worse, so I just smile and offer encouragement. I tell her to stretch it out over two or even three days. That way she won't have to rush so much. I also remind her that missing lunch completely now and then wouldn't hurt her any (if you know what I mean). I like to think tact is one of my strong points.

When doing simple jobs, she seems to think she needs more rest periods. She had to take a break when she was only half finished mowing the lawn. I try not to make a scene. I'm a fair man. I tell her to fix herself a nice, big, cold glass of freshly squeezed lemonade and just sit for a while and, as long as she is making one for herself, she may as well make one for me too.

Love and Marriage ...

I know that I probably look like a saint in the way I support her. I'm not saying that showing this much consideration is easy. Many men will find it difficult. Some will find it impossible! Nobody knows better than I do how frustrated women get, as they get older. However, guys, even if you just use a little more tact and less criticism of your aging wife because of this article, I will consider that writing this was well worthwhile.
After all, we are put on this earth to help each other.

Sincerely,

Kevin

EDITOR'S NOTE:
Kevin died suddenly on March 1 of a perforated rectum. The police report says he was found with a Calloway extra long 50-inch Big Bertha Driver II golf club jammed up his rear end, with barely 5 inches of grip showing and a sledge hammer laying nearby.

His wife was arrested and charged with murder. The all-woman jury took only 15 minutes to find her Not Guilty, accepting her defence that Kevin somehow, without looking, accidentally sat down on his golf club

Love and Marriage ...

THE 5 SECRETS

OF A PERFECT RELATIONSHIP

1 It's important to have a woman who helps at home, cooks, cleans an has a job.

2 It's important to have a woman who can make you laugh.

3 It's important to have a woman you can trust and who would never lie.

4 It's important to have a woman who is good in bed, and likes being with you.

but

5 It's absolutely vital that these four women don't know each other.

Love and Marriage ...

To my darling husband,

Before you return from your overseas trip I just want to let you know about the small accident I had with the pick-up truck when I turned into the driveway.

Fortunately not too bad and I really didn't get hurt, so please don't worry too much about me. I was coming home from Sylvia Park and when I turned into the driveway I accidentally pushed down on the accelerator instead of the brake. The garage door is slightly bent but the pick-up fortunately came to a halt when it bumped into your car.

I am really sorry, but I know with your kind-hearted personality you will forgive me. You know how much I love you and care for you my sweetheart.

I am enclosing a picture for you.

I cannot wait to hold you in my arms again.
Your loving wife XX

Love and Marriage ...

P.S. Your girlfriend phoned.

Love and Marriage ...

APPLICATION FOR A NIGHT OUT WITH THE BOYS

Name of Boyfriend/Fiancé/Husband:

I request permission for a leave of absence from the **highest authority** in my life for the following period:

Date: _____   Time of departure: _____   Time of return NOT to exceed: _____

Should permission be granted, I do solemnly swear to only visit the locations stated below, at the stated times. I agree to refrain from hitting on or flirting with other women. I shall not even speak to another female, except as expressly permitted in writing below. I will not turn off my mobile after two pints, nor shall I consume above the allowed volume of alcohol without first phoning for a taxi AND calling you for a verbal waiver of said alcohol allowance. I understand that even if permission is granted to go out, my girlfriend/fiancé/wife retains the right to be pissed off with me the following week for no valid reason whatsoever.

Amount of alcohol allowed (units)   Beer ___   Wine ___   Liquor ___   Total ___

Locations to be visited
Location: ___   From: ___   To: ___
Location: ___   From: ___   To: ___
Location: ___   From: ___   To: ___

Females with whom conversation is permitted _____

IMPORTANT – STRIPPER CLAUSE: Notwithstanding the female contact permitted above, I promise to refrain from coming within one hundred (100) feet of a stripper or exotic dancer. Violation of this Stripper Clause shall be grounds for immediate termination of the relationship.

I acknowledge my position in life. I know who wears the trousers in our relationship, and I agree it's not me. I promise to abide by your rules & regulations. I understand that this is going to cost me a fortune in chocolates & flowers. You reserve the right to obtain and use my credit cards whenever you wish to do so. I hereby promise to take you to a Michael Bolton concert, should I not return home by the approved time. On my way home, I will not pick a fight with any stranger, nor shall I conduct in depth discussions with the said entity. Upon my return home, I promise not to urinate anywhere other than in the toilet. In addition, I will refrain from waking you up, breathing my vile breath in your face, and attempting to breed like a (drunken) rabbit.

I declare that to the best of my knowledge (of which I have none compared to my **BETTER** half), the above information is correct.
Signed - Boyfriend/Fiancé/Husband: _____

Request is: APPROVED ___   **DENIED** ___

This decision is not negotiable. If approved, cut permission slip below and carry at all times.
✂...
Permission for my boyfriend/fiancé/husband to be away for the following period of time:
Date: ___   Time of departure: ___   Time of return: ___

Signed – Girlfriend/Fiancé/Wife: _____

Love and Marriage ...

APPLICATION FOR A NIGHT OUT WITH THE GIRLS

Name of Girlfriend/Fiancé/Partner/Wife: _____

I'm going out.

Signed: (me) _____

Battle of the Sexes

DICTIONARY FOR WOMEN'S PERSONAL ADS

40-ish	= 49
Adventurous	= Slept with everyone
Athletic	= No tits
Average looking	= Ugly
Beautiful	= Pathological liar
Contagious Smile	= Does a lot of pills
Emotionally secure	= On medication
Feminist	= Fat
Free spirit	= Junkie
Friendship first	= Former very *friendly* person
Fun	= Annoying
Open-minded	= Desperate
Outgoing	= Loud and Embarrassing
Passionate	= Sloppy drunk
Professional	= Bitch
Voluptuous	= Very Fat
Large frame	= Hugely Fat
Wants Soul mate	= Stalker

Battle of the Sexes

WOMEN'S ENGLISH

Yes	= No
No	= Yes
Maybe	= No
We need	= I want
I am sorry	= you'll be sorry
We need to talk	= you're in trouble
Sure, go ahead	= you better not
Do what you want	= you will pay for this later
I am not upset	= of course I am upset, you moron!
You're very attentive tonight	= is sex all you ever think about?

Battle of the Sexes

MEN'S ENGLISH

I am hungry	= I am hungry
I am sleepy	= I am sleepy
I am tired	= I am tired
Nice dress	= Nice cleavage!
I love you	= let's have sex now
I am bored	= Do you want to have sex?
May I have this dance?	= I'd like to have sex with you
Can I call you sometime?	= I'd like to have sex with you
Do you want to go to a movie?	= I'd like to have sex with you
Can I take you out to dinner?	= I'd like to have sex with you
Those shoes don't go with that outfit	= I'm gay

SHOW THIS TO A MAN WHO NEEDS A LAUGH
AND A WOMAN WITH A SENSE OF HUMOUR!

Battle of the Sexes

I'm not sure who this is,
But she claims she knows you!

A CABBIE PICKS UP A NUN

She gets into the cab, and notices that the VERY handsome
cab driver won't stop staring at her.
She asks him why he is staring.
He replies, 'I have a question to ask you but I don't want to
offend you.'

She answers, 'My son, you cannot offend me. When you're as old as
I am and have been a nun as long as I have, you get a chance to see
and hear just about everything. I'm sure that there's nothing you
could say or ask that I would find offensive.'

'Well, I've always had a fantasy to have a nun kiss me.'

She responds, 'Well, let's see what we can do about that:
1. You have to be single
and
2 . You must be Catholic.'

The cab driver is very excited and says,

'Yes, I'm single and Catholic!'

'OK' the nun says. 'Pull into the next alley.'

The nun fulfils his fantasy, with a kiss that would make a hooker blush. But when they get back on the road, the cab driver starts crying ...
'My dear child,' says the Nun, 'why are you crying?'

'Forgive me but I've sinned. I lied and I must confess, I'm married and I'm Jewish.'

The Nun says, 'That's OK. My name is Kevin and I'm going to a fancy dress party'

Religion Can be Funny

Can you imagine the nun sitting at her desk grading these papers, all the while trying to keep a straight face and maintain her composure!

PAY SPECIAL ATTENTION TO THE WORDING AND SPELLING. IF YOU KNOW THE BIBLE EVEN A LITTLE, YOU'LL FIND THIS HILARIOUS! IT COMES FROM A CATHOLIC ELEMENTARY SCHOOL TEST.

KIDS WERE ASKED QUESTIONS ABOUT THE OLD AND NEW TESTAMENTS. THE FOLLOWING STATEMENTS ABOUT THE BIBLE WERE WRITTEN BY CHILDREN. THEY HAVE NOT BEEN RETOUCHED OR CORRECTED. INCORRECT SPELLING HAS BEEN LEFT IN.

1.   IN THE FIRST BOOK OF THE BIBLE, GUINESSIS. GOD
        GOT TIRED OF CREATING THE WORLD SO HE TOOK
        THE SABBATH OFF.

2.   ADAM AND EVE WERE CREATED FROM AN APPLE TREE.
        NOAH'S WIFE WAS JOAN OF ARK. NOAH BUILT AND ARK
        AND THE ANIMALS CAME ON IN PEARS.

3.   LOTS WIFE WAS A PILLAR OF SALT DURING THE DAY,
        BUT A BALL OF FIRE DURING THE NIGHT.

4.   THE JEWS WERE A PROUD PEOPLE AND THROUGHOUT
        HISTORY THEY HAD TROUBLE WITH UNSYMPATHETIC
        GENITALS.

5.   SAMPSON WAS A STRONGMAN WHO LET HIMSELF BE LED
        ASTRAY BY A JEZEBEL LIKE DELILAH.

6.   SAMSON SLAYED THE PHILISTINES WITH THE AXE OF
      THE APOSTLES.

7.   MOSES LED THE JEWS TO THE RED SEA WHERE THEY
      MADE UNLEAVENED BREAD WHICH IS BREAD WITHOUT
      ANY INGREDIENTS.

8.   THE EGYPTIANS WERE ALL DROWNED IN THE DESSERT.
      AFTERWARDS, MOSES WENT UP TO MOUNT CYANIDE
      TO GET THE TEN COMMANDMENTS

9.   THE FIRST COMMANDMENTS WAS WHEN EVE TOLD ADAM
      TO EAT THE APPLE.

10.   THE SEVENTH COMMANDMENT IS THOU SHALT NOT ADMIT
      ADULTERY.

11.   MOSES DIED BEFORE HE EVER REACHED CANADA THEN
      JOSHUA LED THE HEBREWS IN THE BATTLE OF GERITOL.

12.   THE GREATEST MIRICLE IN THE BIBLE IS WHEN JOSHUA
      TOLD HIS SON TO STAND STILL AND HE OBEYED HIM.

13.   DAVID WAS A HEBREW KING WHO WAS SKILLED AT PLAY-
      ING THE LIAR. HE FOUGHT THE FINKELSTEINS, A RACE OF
      PEOPLE WHO LIVED IN BIBLICAL TIMES.

14.   SOLOMON, ONE OF DAVIDS SONS, HAD 300 WIVES AND
      700 PORCUPINES.

15.   WHEN MARY HEARD SHE WAS THE MOTHER OF JESUS, SHE
      SANG THE MAGNA CARTA.

Religion Can be Funny

16. WHEN THE THREE WISE GUYS FROM THE EAST SIDE ARRIVED THEY FOUND JESUS IN THE MANAGER.

17. JESUS WAS BORN BECAUSE MARY HAD AN IMMACULATE CONTRAPTION.

18. ST. JOHN THE BLACKSMITH DUMPED WATER ON HIS HEAD.

19. JESUS ENUNCIATED THE GOLDEN RULE, WHICH SAYS TO DO UNTO OTHERS BEFORE THEY DO ONE TO YOU. HE ALSO EXPLAINED A MAN DOTH NOT LIVE BY SWEAT ALONE.

20. IT WAS A MIRICLE WHEN JESUS ROSE FROM THE DEAD AND MANAGED TO GET THE TOMBSTONE OFF THE ENTRANCE.

21. THE PEOPLE WHO FOLLOWED THE LORD WERE CALLED THE 12 DECIBELS.

22. THE EPISTELS WERE THE WIVES OF THE APOSTLES.

23. ONE OF THE OPPOSSUMS WAS ST. MATTHEW WHO WAS ALSO A TAXIMAN.

24. ST. PAUL CAVORTED TO CHRISTIANITY, HE PREACHED HOLY ACRIMONY WHICH IS ANOTHER NAME FOR MARRAIGE.

25. CHRISTIANS HAVE ONLY ONE SPOUSE. THIS IS CALLED MONOTONY.

Religion Can be Funny

Here's your first Christmas Joke! (it's a groaner, sorry)

THE FIRST CHRISTMAS JOKE ...

Three men died on Christmas Eve and were met by Saint Peter at the pearly gates.
'In honour of this holy season' Saint Peter said, 'You must each possess something that symbolizes Christmas to get into heaven.'

The first man fumbled through his pockets and pulled out a lighter. He flicked it on. 'It represents a candle', he said.
'You may pass through the pearly gates' Saint Peter said.

The second man reached into his pocket and pulled out a set of keys. He shook them and said, 'They're bells.' Saint Peter said 'You may pass through the pearly gates'.

The third man started searching desperately through his pockets and finally pulled out a pair of women's panties.
St. Peter looked at the man with a raised eyebrow and asked, 'And just what do those symbolize?'
The man replied, 'These are Carols.'

And So The Christmas Season Begins......

Religion Can be Funny

A Jewish congregation in suburban Boston honors its Rabbi for 25 years of service by sending him to Hawaii for a week, all expenses paid.

When he walks into his hotel room, he finds a beautiful nude woman lying on the bed. She greets the Rabbi with, 'Hi, Rabbi, I'm a little something extra that the President of the Temple arranged for you.'

The Rabbi is incensed. He picks up the phone, calls the President of the Temple and shouts, 'Greenblatt, what were you thinking? Where is your respect? I am the moral leader of our religious community! I am very angry with you and you have not heard the end of this.'

Hearing this, the naked woman gets up and starts to get dressed. The Rabbi turns to her and asks, 'Where are you going? I'm not angry with you.'

PERILS OF A CATHOLIC UPBRINGING

As I walked down the busy sidewalk, knowing I was late for Mass, my eye fell upon one of those unfortunate, homeless vagabonds that are found in every city these days.

Some people turned to stare. Others quickly looked away as if the sight would somehow contaminate them.

Recalling my old pastor, Father Mike, who always admonished me to 'care for the sick, feed the hungry and clothe the naked,' I was moved by some powerful inner urge to reach out to this unfortunate person.

Wearing what can only be described as rags, carrying every worldly possession in two plastic bags, my heart was touched by this person's condition. Yes, where some people saw only rags, I saw a true, hidden beauty.

A small voice inside my head called out, 'Reach out, reach out and touch this person!'

So I did ....

Religion Can be Funny

... I won't be at Mass this week.

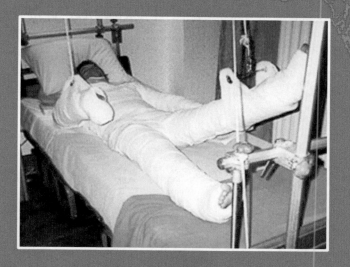

Religion Can be Funny

A soldier ran up to a nun. Out of breath he asked, 'Please, may I hide under your skirt. I'll explain later.'

The nun agreed. A moment later two Military Police ran up and asked, 'Sister, have you seen a soldier?'

The nun replied, 'He went that way.'

After the MPs ran off, the soldier crawled out from under her skirt and said, 'I can't thank you enough Sister. You see, I don't want to go to Iraq.'

The nun said, 'I understand completely.'

The soldier added, 'I hope I'm not rude, but you have a great pair of legs!'

The nun replied, 'If you had looked a little higher, you would have seen a great pair of balls....I don't want to go to Iraq either.'

THE 4 JEWISH BROTHERS

Four Jewish brothers left home for college, and they became successful doctors, and lawyers and prospered. Some years later, they chatted after having dinner together. They discussed the gifts that they were able to give to their elderly mother who lived far away in another city.

The first said, 'I had a big house built for Mama.'

The second said, 'I had a hundred thousand dollar theater builtin the house.'

The third said, 'I had my Mercedes dealer deliver her an SL600 with a chauffeur.'

The fourth said, 'Listen to this. You know how Mama loved reading the Torah and you know she can't anymore because she can't see very well. I met this Rabbi who told me about a parrot that can recite the entire Torah. It took twenty rabbis 12 years to teach him. I had to pledge to contribute $100,000 a year for twenty years to the temple, but it was worth it. Mama just has to name the chapter and verse and the parrot will recite it.'

The other brothers were impressed.

After the holidays Mom sent out her "Thank You" notes. She wrote:

Milton Bubelle, The house you built is so huge. I live in only one room, but I have to clean the whole house. Thanks anyway.

Marvin Main Shene Kinde, I am too old to travel. I stay home, I have my groceries delivered, so I never use the Mercedes ... and the driver you hired is a Nazi. The thought was good. Thanks.

Menachim Tataleh, You give me an expensive theater with Dolby sound, it could hold 50 people, but all my friends are dead, I've lost my hearing and I'm nearly blind. I'll never use it. Thank you for the gesture just the same.

Dearest Melvin, You were the only son to have the good sense to give a little thought to your gift. Thank you!

... The chicken was delicious.

Religion Can be Funny

NOAH TODAY

In the year 2012, the Lord came unto Noah,Who was now living in Macclesfield, England and said:
'Once again, the earth has become wicked and over-populated, and I see the end of all flesh before me. Build another Ark and save 2 of every living thing. Along with a few good humans.'

He gave Noah the blueprints, saying:
'You have 6 months to build the Ark before I will start the unending rain for 40 days and 40 nights.'

Six months later, the Lord looked down and saw Noah Weeping in his yard - but no Ark.
'Noah!,' He roared, 'I'm about to start the rain! Where is the Ark?'

'Forgive me, Lord,' begged Noah, 'but things have changed ... I needed a Building Permit. I've been arguing with the Boat Inspector about the need for a sprinkler system. My neighbours claim that I've violated the Neighbourhood Bye-Laws by building the Ark in my back garden and exceeding the height limitations. We had to go to the Local Planning Committee for a decision.'

"Then the Local Council and the Electricity Company demanded a shed load of money for the future costs of moving power lines and other overhead obstructions, to clear the passage for the Ark's move to the sea. I told them that the sea would be coming to us, but they would hear nothing of it.'

'Getting the wood was another problem. There's a ban on cutting local trees in order to save the Greater Spotted Barn Owl. I tried to convince the environmentalists that I Needed the wood to save the owls - but no go!'

Religion Can be Funny

'

When I started gathering the animals the RSPCA took me to court. They insisted that I was confining wild animals against their will. They argued the accommodations were too restrictive, and it was cruel and inhumane to put so many animals in a confined space.'

'Then the Environmental Agency ruled that I couldn't build the Ark until they'd conducted an environmental impact study on your proposed flood.'

'I'm still trying to resolve a complaint with the Human Rights Commission on how many minorities I'm supposed to hire for my building crew.'

'Immigration are checking the Visa status of most of the people who want to work.'

'The trades unions say I can't use my sons. They insist I have to hire only Union workers with Ark-building experience.'

'To make matters worse, the Inland Revenue seized all my assets, claiming I'm trying to leave the country illegally with endangered species.'

'So, forgive me, Lord, but it would take at least 10
Years for me to finish this Ark.'

Suddenly the skies cleared, the sun began to shine, and a rainbow stretched across the sky. Noah looked up in wonder and asked:

'You mean you're not going to destroy the world?'

'No,' said the Lord. 'Gordon Brown and the Government beat me to it.'

SYNAGOGUE BULLETIN BLOOPERS

All the mistakes in spelling and typing were left in. These announcements were found in synagogue newsletters and bulletins. Even spell check wouldn't have helped.

- Don't let worry kill you. Let your synagogue help. Join us for our Oneg after services. Prayer and medication to follow. Remember in prayer the many who are sick of our congregation.

- For those of you who have children and don't know it, we have a nursery downstairs.

- We are pleased to announce the birth of David Weiss, the sin of Rabbi and Mrs. Abe Weiss.

- Thursday at 12.30, there will be a meeting of the Little Mothers Club. All women wishing to become Little Mothers please see the rabbi in his private study.

- The ladies of Hadassah have cast off clothing of every kind and they may be seen in the basement on Tuesdays.

- A bean supper will be held Wednesday evening in the community center. Music will follow.

Religion Can be Funny

- Weight Watchers will meet at 7 PM at the JCC. Please use the large double door at the side entrance.

- Rabbi is on vacation. Massages can be given to his secretary.

- Goldblum will be entering the hospital this week for testes.

- The Men's Club is warmly invited to the Oneg hosted by Hadassah. Refreshments will be served for a nominal feel.

- Please join us as we show our support for Amy and Rob, who are preparing for the girth of their first child.

- We are taking up a collection to defray the cost of the new carpet in the sanctuary. All those wishing to do something on the carpet will come forward and get a piece of paper.

- If you enjoy sinning, the choir is looking for you!

- The Associate Rabbi unveiled the synagogue's new fund raising campaign slogan this week: "I Upped My Pledge. Up yours."

SIPPING VODKA

A new priest at his first mass was so nervous he could hardly speak.

After mass he asked the monsignor how he had done.

The monsignor replied, 'When I am worried about getting nervous on the pulpit, I put a glass of vodka next to the water glass. If I start to get nervous, I take a sip.'

So next Sunday he took the monsignor's advice.

At the beginning of the sermon, he got nervous and took a drink. He proceeded to talk up a storm.

Upon his return to his office after the mass, he found the following note on the door:

1) Sip the vodka, don't gulp.

2) There are 10 commandments, not 12.

3) There are 12 disciples, not 10.

4) Jesus was consecrated, not constipated.

5) Jacob wagered his donkey, he did not bet his ass.

6) We do not refer to Jesus Christ as the late J.C.

Religion Can be Funny

7) The Father, Son, and Holy Ghost are not referred to as Daddy, Junior and the spook.

8) David slew Goliath, he did not kick the sh*t out of him.

9) When David was hit by a rock and was knocked off his donkey, don't say he was stoned off his ass.

10) We do not refer to the cross as the 'Big T.'

11) When Jesus broke the bread at the last supper he said, 'take this and eat it for it is my body.' He did not say 'Eat me'.

12) The Virgin Mary is not called 'Mary with the Cherry'.

13) The recommended grace before a meal is not: Rub-A-Dub-Dub thanks for the grub, Yeah God.

14) Next Sunday there will be a taffy pulling contest at St Peter's not a peter pulling contest at St Taffy's.

JUST PLAIN FUN

Amazing and Stunning Pictures from 2012
World Submarine Racing Championships

JUST PLAIN FUN

Well, what did you expect to see?

I said this is Submarine Racing!

JUST PLAIN FUN

Ladies and Gentlemen,
Good evening and welcome to
the 2012 Construction Awards ...

Nominees are ...

1)

2)

JUST PLAIN FUN

3)

4)

5)

6)

JUST PLAIN FUN

7)

8)

9)

JUST PLAIN FUN

10)

11)

JUST PLAIN FUN

and the winner is ...

JUST PLAIN FUN

Ever wondered what happens when Greeting Card writers are having a bad day ...

My tyre was thumping.
I thought it was flat
When I looked at the tyre...
I noticed your cat.
Sorry!

Heard your wife left you
How upset you must be.
But don't fret about it...
She's moved in with me.

Congratulations on your wedding day!
Too bad no one likes your husband.

How could two people as beautiful as you
Have such an ugly baby?

JUST PLAIN FUN

I've always wanted to have
someone to hold , someone
to love.
After having met you ..
I've changed my mind.

·

I must admit , you brought Religion into my life.
I never believed in Hell until I met you.

·

As the days go by , I think of how lucky I am......
That you're not here to ruin it for me.

·

Congratulations on your promotion.
Before you go...
Would you like to take this knife out of my back?
You'll probably need it again.

·

Happy Birthday, Uncle Dad! (Available
only in Tennessee, Arkansas, Kentucky
and West Virginia)

·

JUST PLAIN FUN

Happy birthday! You look great for your age.
Almost Lifelike!

.

When we were together ,
you always said you'd die for me.
Now that we've broken up ,
I think it's time you kept your promise.

.

We have been friends for a very long time ..
let's say we stop?

.

I'm so miserable without you
it's almost like you're here.

JUST PLAIN FUN

Congratulations on your new bundle of joy.
Did you ever find out who the father was?

Your friends and I wanted to do
something special for your birthday.
So we're having you put to sleep.

So your daughter's a hooker, and it spoiled your day.
Look at the bright side ,
it's really good pay

JUST PLAIN FUN

First Book of Government

PSALM 2012

Obama is the shepherd I did not want.
He leadeth me beside the still factories.
He restoreth my faith in the Republican party.
He guideth me in the path of unemployment for his party's sake.
Yea, though I walk through the valley of the bread line,
I shall fear no hunger for his bailouts are with me.
He has anointed my income with taxes,
My expenses runneth over.
Surely, poverty and hard living will follow me all the days of my life,
And I will live in a mortgaged home forever.
I am glad I am American,
I am glad that I am free.
But I wish I were a dog,
And Obama was a tree

JUST PLAIN FUN

This is a joke that is supposed to bring you luck.

An elderly woman walked into the Bank of Canada one morning with a purse full of money. She wanted to open a savings account and insisted on talking to the president of the Bank because, she said, she had a lot of money.

After many lengthy discussions (after all, the client is always right) an employee took the elderly woman to the president's office. The president of the Bank asked her how much she wanted to deposit. She placed her purse on his desk and replied, '$165,000'. The president was curious and asked her how she had been able to save so much money. The elderly woman replied that she made bets.

The president was surprised and asked, 'What kind of bets?' The elderly woman replied, 'Well, I bet you $25,000 that your testicles are square.'
The president started to laugh and told the woman that it was impossible to win a bet like that. The woman never batted an eye. She just looked at the president and said, 'Would you like to take my bet?'
'Certainly', replied the president. 'I bet you $25,000 that my testicles are not square.'
'Done', the elderly woman answered. 'But given the amount of money involved, if you don't mind I would like to come back at 10 o' clock tomorrow morning with my lawyer as a witness.'
'No problem', said the president of the Bank confidently.

JUST PLAIN FUN

That night, the president became very nervous about the bet and spent a long time in front of the mirror examining his testicles, turning them this way and that, checking them over again and a gain until he was positive that no one could consider his testicles as square and reassuring himself that there was no way he could lose the bet.

The next morning at exactly 10 o'clock the elderly woman arrived at the president's office with her lawyer and acknowledged the $25,000 bet made the day before that the president's testicles were square.

The president confirmed that the bet was the same as the one made the day before. Then the elderly woman asked him to drop his pants etc. so that she and her lawyer could see clearly.
The president was happy to oblige. The elderly woman came closer so she could see better and asked the president if she could touch them. 'Of course', said the president. 'Given the amount of money involved, you should be 100% sure.'

The elderly woman did so with a little smile. Suddenly the president noticed that the lawyer was banging his head against the wall. He asked the elderly woman why he was doing that and she replied, 'Oh, it's probably because I bet him $100,000 that around 10 o'clock in the morning I would be holding the balls of the President of the Bank of Canada!'

JUST PLAIN FUN

Your House As Seen By:

You

Your Buyer

JUST PLAIN FUN

Your Lender

Your Mortgage Valuer

Your Council Tax Assessor

JUST PLAIN FUN

You just couldn't make this up ...

Teatime love bite

A WOMAN almost bit off her husband's willy as he cooked pancakes for tea — while she gave him oral sex.

In the heat of passion he lost his grip on the pan and spilt boiling oil down her naked back.

She clenched her teeth on his willy and in agony he bashed her on the head with the pan.

Both only admitted how they received their injuries after "intense questioning" by hospital docs in Carioca, Romania.

The man needed treatment to his willy while the wife had burns, two black eyes and a broken cheek bone.

Swimmer trapped by beach balls

A MAN got a nasty surprise when he tried to get out of his deckchair and found his testicles had become stuck between two slats of wood. Mario Visnjic had been swimming naked off Valalta beach in Croatia and his testicles had shrunk in the cool sea. When he sat down they slipped through the slats and then, as he lay in the sun, expanded back to normal size. He was freed after he called beach maintenance services on his mobile phone and they sent a member of staff to cut the deckchair in half.

Buzzing undies make shopper faint

A WOMAN collapsed in a supermarket when her vibrating panties made her faint with pleasure.

The kinky 33-year-old housewife was wearing a pair of battery-operated Passion Pants, bought from a sex shop, while she did her shopping, according to the British tabloid The Sun.

But she got so stimulated by the 6cm vibrating bullet in the panties that she lost consciousness.

She fell and hit her head in the crowded supermarket in Swansea, Wales.

When paramedics arrived, they found her black imitation leather knickers still buzzing.

They took them off before an ambulance took her to hospital.

The woman, whose identity has been kept private, suffered no long-lasting ill-effects.

And as she left the hospital, a paramedic gave her back the Passion Pants in a plastic bag.

A spokesman for the Asda supermarket chain told The Sun: "We like to think shopping with us is exciting enough already."

WHY WE LIKE THE BRITISH

FROM BRITISH NEWSPAPERS

- Commenting on a complaint from a Mr. Arthur Purdey about a large gas bill, a spokesman for North West Gas said, 'We agree it was rather high for the time of year. It's possible Mr. Purdey has been charged for the gas used up during the explosion that destroyed his house.'
(The Daily Telegraph)

- Irish police are being handicapped in a search for a stolen van because they cannot issue a description. It's a Special Branch vehicle and they don't want the public to know what it looks like.
(The Guardian)

- A young girl who was blown out to sea on a set of inflatable teeth was rescued by a man on an inflatable lobster. A coast guard spokesman commented, 'This sort of thing is all too common'.
(The Times)

- At the height of the gale, the harbourmaster radioed a coastguard and asked him to estimate the wind speed. He replied he was sorry, but he didn't have a gauge. However, if it was any help, the wind had just blown his Land Rover off the cliff.
(Aberdeen Evening Express)

- Mrs. Irene Graham of Thorpe Avenue , Boscombe, delighted the audience with her reminiscence of the German prisoner of war who was sent each week to do her garden. He was repatriated at the end of 1945, she recalled. 'He'd always seemed a nice friendly chap, but when the crocuses came up in the middle of our lawn in February 1946, they spelt out 'Heil Hitler."
(Bournemouth Evening Echo)

A list of actual announcements that London Tube train drivers have made to their passengers...

- 'Ladies and Gentlemen, I do apologize for the delay to your service. I know you're all dying to get home, unless, of course, you happen to be married to my ex-wife, in which case you'll want to cross over to the Westbound and go in the opposite direction.'

- 'Your delay this evening is caused by the line controller suffering from E & B syndrome: not knowing his elbow from his backside. I'll let you know any further information as soon as I'm given any. '

- 'Do you want the good news first or the bad news? The good news is that last Friday was my birthday and I hit the town and had a great time. The bad news is that there is a points failure somewhere between Stratford and East Ham, which means we probably won't reach our destination.'

- 'Ladies and gentlemen, we apologize for the delay, but there is a security alert at Victoria station and we are therefore stuck here for the foreseeable future, so let's take our minds off it and pass some time together. All together now ... 'Ten green bottles, hanging on a wall ...'

- 'We are now travelling through Baker Street .. As you can see, Baker Street is closed. It would have been nice if they had actually told me, so I could tell you earlier, but no, they don't think about things like that'.

- 'Beggars are operating on this train. Please do NOT encourage these professional beggars. If you have any spare change, please give it to a registered charity. Failing that, give it to me.'

- During an extremely hot rush hour on the Central Line, the driver announced in a West Indian drawl: 'Step right this way for the sauna, ladies and gentleman... Unfortunately, towels are not provided.'

- 'Let the passengers off the train FIRST!'(pause). 'Oh go on then, stuff yourselves in like sardines, see if I care - I'm going home ...'

- 'Please allow the doors to close. Try not to confuse this with 'Please hold the doors open.' The two are distinct and separate instructions.'

- 'Please note that the beeping noise coming from the doors means that the doors are about to close. It does not mean throw yourself or your bags into the doors.'

JUST PLAIN FUN

- 'We can't move off because some idiot has their hand stuck in the door.'

- 'To the gentleman wearing the long grey coat trying to get on the second carriage - what part of 'stand clear of the doors' don't you understand?'

- 'Please move all baggage away from the doors.' (...pause). 'Please move ALL belongings away from the doors.' (...pause). 'This is a personal message to the man in the brown suit wearing glasses at the rear of the train: Put the pie down, four-eyes, and move your bl**dy golf clubs away from the door before I come down there and shove them up your a**e sideways!'

- 'May I remind all passengers that there is strictly no smoking allowed on any part of the Underground. However, if you are smoking a joint, it's only fair that you pass it round the rest of the carriage.'

WHO IS JACK SCHITT?

For some time many of us have wondered just who is Jack Schitt. We find ourselves at a loss when someone says:

'You don't know Jack Schitt!'

Well, thanks to this geneaology research, you can now respond in an intellectual way.

Jack Schitt is the only son of Awe Schitt, the fertiliser magnate who married O. Schitt, the owner of Knee-Deep N.Schitt, Inc. They had one son, Jack.

In turn, Jack Schitt married Noe Schitt. The deeply religious couple produced six children: Holy Schitt, Giva Schitt, Fulla Schitt, Bull Schitt, and the twins Deep Schitt and Dip Schitt.

Against her parents' objections, Deep Schitt married Dumb Schitt, a high school dropout. Meanwhile, Deep Schitt married Loada Schitt, and they produced a son with a rather nervous disposition named Chicken Schitt.

Two of the other six children, Fulla Schitt and Giva Schitt, were inseparable throughout childhood and subsequently married the Happens brothers in a dual ceremony.

JUST PLAIN FUN

The wedding announcement in the local newspaper announced the Schitt-Happens nuptials.

The Schitt-Happens children were Dawg, Byrd, and Horse.

Bull Schitt, the prodigal son, left home to tour the world.

He recently returned from Italy with his new Italian bride, Pisa Schitt.

Now, when someone says 'You don't know Jack Schitt', you can correct them.

P.S. Bull and Pisa Schitt have recently produced a little bruiser son, Tuff!

JUST PLAIN FUN

We all know people like this, don't we?

Idiotic 'Millionaire' Contestant Makes Worst Use Of Lifelines Ever

Kathy Evans, the single dumbest contestant to ever get on 'Who Wants To Be A Millionaire?'

NEW YORK - Idaho resident Kathy Evans brought humiliation to her friends and family Tuesday when she set a new standard for stupidity with her appearance on the popular TV show, 'Who Wants To Be A Millionaire.'

It seems that Evans, a 32-year-old wife and mother of two, got stuck on the first question, and proceeded to make what fans of the show are dubbing 'the absolute worst use of lifelines ever.'

After being introduced to the show's host Meredith Vieira, Evans assured her that she was ready to play, whereupon she was posed with an extremely easy $100 question. The question was:

'Which of the following is the largest?'
A) A Peanut
B) An Elephant
C) The Moon
D) Hey, who you calling large?

JUST PLAIN FUN

Immediately Mrs. Evans was struck with an all consuming
as she realized that this was a question to which she
did not readily know the answer.

"Hmm, oh boy, that's a toughie,' said Evans, as Vieira did her
level best to hide her disbelief and disgust. 'I mean, I'm sure
heard of some of these things before, but I have no idea they
would be.'

Having made the decision to use the first of her three lifelines, the 50/50. Answers A and D were removed, leaving
her to decide which was bigger, an elephant or the moon.
However, faced with an incredibly easy question, Evans was
still unsure.

"Oh! It removed the two I was leaning towards!' she
exclaimed. "Darn, I think I better phone a friend".
Using the second of her two lifelines on the first
question, Mrs. Evans asked to be connected with her
friend Betsy, who is an office assistant.

JUST PLAIN FUN

'Hi Betsy! How are you? This is Kathy! I'm on TV!' said Evans, wasting the first seven seconds of her call. 'Ok, I got an important question. Which of the following is the largest? B, an elephant, or C, the moon. 15 seconds hun.'

Betsy quickly replied that the answer was C, the moon. Evans proceeded to argue with her friend for the remaining ten seconds. 'Come on Betsy, are you sure?' said Evans. 'How sure are you? Puh, that can't be it.'

To everyone's astonishment, the moronic Evans declined to take her friend's advice and pick 'The Moon.'
'I just don't know if I can trust Betsy. She's not all that bright. So I think I'd like to ask the audience,' said Evans.

Asked to vote on the correct answer, the audience returned 98% in favor of answer C, 'The Moon.' Having used up all her lifelines, Evans then made the dumbest choice of her life.

'Wow, seems like everybody is against what I'm thinking,' said the too-stupid-to-live Evans. 'But you know, sometimes you just got to go with your gut. So, let's see. For which is larger, an elephant or the moon, I'm going to have to go with B, an elephant.. Final answer.'

Evans sat before the dumbfounded audience, the only one waiting with bated breath, and was told that she was wrong, and that the answer was in fact, C, 'The Moon.'

JUST PLAIN FUN

Two Ladies Talking in Heaven ...

1st woman: Hi! My name is Wanda.

2nd woman: Hi! I'm Sylvia. How'd you die?

1st woman: I froze to death

2nd woman: How horrible!

1st woman: It wasn't so bad. After I quit shaking from the cold, I began to get warm and sleepy, and finally died a peaceful death. What about you?

2nd woman: I died of a massive heart attack. I suspected that my husband was cheating, so I came home early to catch him in the act. But instead, I found him all by himself in the den watching TV.

1st woman: So, what happened?

2nd woman: I was so sure there was another woman there somewhere that I started running all over the house looking. I ran up into the attic and searched, and down into the basement. Then I went through every closet and checked under all the beds. I kept this up until I had looked everywhere, and finally I became so exhausted that I just keeled over with a heart attack and died.

1st woman: Too bad you didn't look in the freezer - we'd both still be alive.

JUST PLAIN FUN

When Grandma Goes To Court

Humor; Posted on: 2008-01-17 20:06:02 [Print / Instant Flyer]

Lawyers should never ask a Mississippi grandma a question if they aren't prepared for the answer.

In a trial, a Southern small-town prosecuting attorney called his first witness, a grandmotherly, elderly woman to the stand. He approached her and asked, 'Mrs. Jones, do you know me?' She responded, 'Why, yes, I do know you, Mr. Williams. I've known you since you were a boy, and frankly, you've been a big disappointment to me. You lie, you cheat on your wife, and you manipulate people and talk about them behind their backs. You think you're a big shot when you haven't the brains to realize you'll never amount to anything more than a two-bit paper pusher. Yes, I know you.'

The lawyer was stunned. Not knowing what else to do, he pointed across the room and asked, 'Mrs. Jones, do you know the defense attorney?'

She again replied, 'Why yes, I do. I've known Mr. Bradley since he was a youngster, too. He's lazy, bigoted, and he has a drinking problem. He can't build a normal relationship with anyone, and his law practice is one of the worst in the entire state. Not to mention he cheated on his wife with three different women. One of them was your wife. Yes, I know him.'

The defense attorney nearly died.

The judge asked both counselors to approach the bench and, in a very quiet voice, said,

'If either of you idiots asks her if she knows me, I'll send you both to the electric chair.'

A woman was admitted to hospital with a vacuum cleaner nozzle wedged up her bum. Although she's in intensive care, the doctors say she is picking up nicely.

2 junkies injected curry powder instead of heroin.....One is in a Korma and the other has a dodgy Tikka!

JUST PLAIN FUN

For all Who Work With Rude Customers ...

An award should go to the Virgin Airlines desk attendant in Sydney some months ago for being smart and funny, while making her point, when confronted with a passenger who probably deserved to fly as cargo.

A crowded Virgin flight was cancelled after Virgin's 767s had been withdrawn from service. A single attendant was rebooking a long line of inconvenienced travellers. Suddenly an angry passenger pushed his way to the desk. He slapped his ticket down on the counter and said, 'I HAVE to be on this flight and it HAS to be FIRST CLASS'.

The attendant replied,'I'm sorry, sir. I'll be happy to try to help you, but I've got to help these people first, and I'm sure we'll be able to work something out.'

The passenger was unimpressed. He asked loudly, so that the passengers behind him could hear, 'DO YOU HAVE ANY IDEA WHO I AM?'

Without hesitating, the attendant smiled and grabbed her public address microphone: 'May I have your attention please, may I have your attention please', she began - her voice heard clearly throughout the terminal – 'we have a passenger here at Desk 14 WHO DOES NOT KNOW WHO HE IS. If anyone can help him find his identity, please come to Desk 14.'

With the folks behind him in line laughing hysterically, the man glared at the Virgin attendant, gritted his teeth and said, 'F**k You!'

Without flinching, she smiled and said, 'I'm sorry, sir, but you'll have to get in line for that too.'

JUST PLAIN FUN

FLOWERS

Two friends, a blonde and a redhead, were walking down the street and passed a flower shop where the redhead saw her boyfriend buying her flowers.

The redhead sighed and said 'Oh crap, my boyfriend is buying me flowers again.'

The blonde looked quizzically at her and said: 'You don't like getting flowers from your boyfriend?'

The redhead replied: 'I love getting flowers, but he always has expectations after giving me flowers, and I just don't feel like spending the next three days on my back with my legs in the air.'

The blonde said, 'Don't you have a vase?'

FIRST TIME SEX

A girl asks her boyfriend to come over Friday night to meet, and have a dinner with her parents.

Since this is such a big event, the girl announces to her boyfriend that after dinner, she would like to go out and make love for the first time. The boy is ecstatic, but he has never had sex before, so he takes a trip to the pharmacist to get some condoms. He tells the pharmacist it's his first time and the pharmacist helps the boy for about an hour. He tells the boy everything there is to know about condoms and sex.

At the register, the pharmacist asks the boy how many condoms he'd like to buy, a 3-pack, 10-pack, or family pack. The boy insists on the family pack because he thinks he will be rather busy, it being his first time and all.

That night, the boy shows up at the girl's parents house and meets his girlfriend at the door. 'Oh, I'm so excited for you to meet my parents, come on in!' The boy goes inside and is taken to the dinner table where the girl's parents are seated. The boy quickly offers to say grace and bows his head. A minute passes, and the boy is still deep in prayer, with his head down.

10 minutes pass, and still no movement from the boy. Finally, after 20 minutes with his head down, the girlfriend leans over and whispers to the boyfriend, 'I had no idea you were this religious.' The boy turns, and whispers back, 'I had no idea your father was a pharmacist'.

JUST PLAIN FUN

MORAL/ETHICAL QUESTION

You are driving down the road in your car on a wild stormy night, when you pass by a bus stop and you see three people waiting for the bus:

1. An old lady who looks as if she is about to die.

2 An old friend who once saved your life.

3. The perfect partner you have been dreaming about.

Which one would you choose to offer a ride to, knowing that there could only be one passenger in your car?

Think seriously about this before you continue reading.

Do you have an answer?

This is a moral/ethical dilemma that was once actually used as part of a job application.

You could pick up the old lady, because she is going to die, and thus you should save her first. Or you could take the old friend because he once saved your life, and this would be the perfect chance to pay him back.

However, you may never be able to find your perfect mate again.

JUST PLAIN FUN

What Human Resources wanted to hear:

The candidate who was hired (out of 200 applicants) had no trouble coming up with his answer. He simply answered:

'I would give the car keys to my old friend and let him take the lady to the hospital. I would stay behind and wait for the bus with the partner of my dreams.'

Sometimes, we gain more if we are able to give up our stubborn thought limitations.

Never forget to 'Think Outside of the Box.'

However ...

HOWEVER ...

The correct answer is to run the old lady over and put her out of her misery, have sex with the perfect partner on the hood of the car, then drive off with the old friend for a few beers.

God, I just love happy endings!

JUST PLAIN FUN

There are many moments of high humour to be found in the formal setting of the Old Bailey. Here are some favorites:

Policeman giving evidence in post office hold up: "I told the suspect: "Armed police, drop your weapon and lie on the floor with your arms outstretched.""

Postmistress later in same trial, gives her version of the events: 'The next thing I know a policeman runs in and shouts: "Drop it you bastard or I'll blow your f**king head off.""

.

Judge after leafing through a bundle of CCTV stills from a bank robbery: 'Which person in the photograph do you say is the defendant'.
Prosecutor: 'The one with the mask and the sawn off shotgun, my Lord.'

.

Barrister quizzing policeman in case of drunk woman accused of dangerous driving and ignoring repeated requests to pull over.'Officer, when you stopped the defendant were your red and blue lights flashing?"
'Yes sir.'
'What did she say?'
'What disco am I at.'

JUST PLAIN FUN

Nervous junior defence barrister quizzing senior pathologist in murder trial: 'Doctor before you performed the autopsy did you check for a pulse.?
'No.'
'Did you check that he was breathing?'
'No.'
'So then it is possible that he was breathing?'
'No.'
'How can you be sure?'
'Because his brain was sitting in a jar on my desk.'
'But could the patient have been alive nevertheless?'

Exasperated doctor: 'it is possible he could have been alive and practising law somewhere.'

.

Barrister in case concerning robbers having gun battle with police, quizzing eye witness: 'You were shot in the fracas?'

Witness: 'No I was shot midway between the fracas and the navel.'

.

Junior prosecutor re examining witness in rape trial:
'Did you say that person in the photograph had a beard?'
'Yes.'
'Would that be a man or a woman?'

JUST PLAIN FUN

Beware of identity theft ...

JUST PLAIN FUN

Computer trouble!

I was having trouble with my computer. So I called Richard, the 11 year old next door whose bedroom looks like Mission Control, and asked him to come over.

Richard clicked a couple of buttons and solved and the problem almost immediately.

As he was walking away, I called after him, 'So, what was wrong?'

He replied, 'It was an ID ten T operator error.'

I didn't want to appear stupid, but nonetheless inquired, 'An, ID ten T operator error? What's that? In case I need to fix it again.'

Richard grinned. 'Haven't you ever heard of an ID ten T operator error before?'

'No,' I replied.

'Write it down,' he said, 'and I think you'll figure it out.'

So I wrote down: I D 1 0 T

I used to like the little shit.

JUST PLAIN FUN

Little Tony was 7 years old and was staying with his grandmother for a few days.

He'd been playing outside with the other kids for a while when he came into the house and asked her: 'Grandma, what's that called when two people sleep in the same room and one is on top of the other?'

She was a little taken aback, but she decided to tell him the truth. 'It's called sex, darling.'

Little Tony said, 'Oh, OK,' and went back outside to play with the other kids.

A few minutes later he came back in and said angrily, 'Grandma, it isn't called sex. It's called Bunk Beds and Jimmy's mom wants to talk to you.'

JUST PLAIN FUN

Only great minds can read this
This is weird, but interesting!

Fi yuo cna raed tihs, yuo hvae a sgtrane mnid too

Cna yuo raed tihs? Olny 55 plepoe out of 100 can.

I cdnuolt blveiee taht I cluod aulaclty uesdnatnrd waht I was rdanieg.

The phaonmneal pweor of the hmuan mnid, aoccdrnig to a rscheearch at Cmabrigde Uinervtisy, it dseno't mtaetr in waht oerdr the ltteres in a wrod are, the olny iproamtnt tihng is taht the frsit and lsat ltteer be in the rghit pclae.

The rset can be a taotl mses and you can sitll raed it whotuit a pboerlm. Tihs is bcuseae the huamn mnid deos not raed ervey lteter by istlef, but the wrod as a wlohe. Azanmig huh? yaeh and I awlyas tghuhot slpeling was ipmorantt! if you can raed tihs forwrad it

JUST PLAIN FUN

A disappointed salesman of Cola returns from his assignment in Israel ...

A friend asked, 'Why weren't you successful with the Israeli's?'

The salesman explained, 'When I got posted in the Middle East , I was very confident that I would make a good sales pitch in rural areas. But, I had a problem I didn't know how to speak Hebrew. So, I planned to convey the message through three posters ...

First poster- A man lying in the hot desert sand...totally exhausted and fainting.

Second poster - man is drinking our Cola.

Third poster- Our man is now totally refreshed.

Then these posters were pasted all over the place
'That should have worked,' said the friend.

The salesman replied 'I didn't realize that the Jews read from right to left!'

JUST PLAIN FUN

A burglar broke into a house one night. He shone his flash-light around, looking for valuables; and when he picked up a CD player to place in his sack, a strange, disembodied voice echoed from the dark saying, 'Jesus is watching you.'

He nearly jumped out of his skin, clicked his flashlight off, and froze. When he heard nothing more after a bit, he shook his head, promised himself a vacation after the next big score, then clicked the light on and began searching for more valuables. Just as he pulled the stereo out so he could dis-connect the wires, Clear as a bell he heard,'Jesus is watching you.'

Freaked out, he shone his light around frantically, looking for the source of the voice. Finally, in the corner of the room, his flashlight beam came to rest on a parrot.

'Did you say that?' he hissed at the parrot.

'Yep,' the parrot confessed, then squawked, 'I'm just trying to warn you.'

The burglar relaxed. 'Warn me, huh? Who in the world are you?'

'Moses,' replied the bird.

'Moses?' the burglar laughed. 'What kind of people would name a bird Moses?'

'The kind of people that would name a Rottweiler Jesus.'

JUST PLAIN FUN

The phone rings and the lady of the house answers, 'Hello Mrs. Sanders, please.'

'Speaking.'

'Mrs. Sanders, this is Doctor at Saint Agnes Laboratory. When your husband's doctor sent his biopsy to the lab last week, a biopsy from another Mr Sanders arrived as well. We are now uncertain which one belongs to your husband. Frankly, either way the results are not too good.'

'What do you mean?' Mrs. Sanders asks nervously.

'Well, one of the specimens tested positive for Alzheimer's and the other one tested positive for HIV. We can't tell which is which.'

'That's dreadful! Can you do the test again?' questioned Mrs. Sanders.

'Normally we can, but Medicare will only pay for these expensive tests one time.'

'Well, what am I supposed to do now?'

'The folks at Medicare recommend that you drop your husband off somewhere in the middle of town. If he finds his way home, don't sleep with him.'

JUST PLAIN FUN

A petrol station owner was trying to increase his sales.
So, he put up a sign that read,

'Free Sex with Fill-Up.'

Soon Fred pulled in, filled his tank and asked for his free
sex. The owner told him to pick a number from 1 to 10. If he
guessed correctly, he would get his free sex.

Fred guessed 8, and the proprietor said, 'You were close. The
number was 7. Sorry.. No sex this time.'

A week later, Fred, along with his friend Bill, pulled in for
another fill-up. Again he asked for his free sex. The proprietor again gave him the same story, and asked him to guess
the correct number.

Fred guessed 2 this time. The proprietor said, 'Sorry, it was 3.
You were close, but no free sex this time.'

As they were driving away, Bill said to Mick, 'I think that game
is rigged and he doesn't really give away free sex.'

Fred replied, 'No it ain't, Bill. It's not rigged at all.
My wife won twice last week.'

JUST PLAIN FUN

A very pretty young speech therapist was getting nowhere with her Stammerers Action group. She had tried every technique in the book without the slightest success.

Finally, thoroughly exasperated, she said 'If any of you can tell me the name of the town where you were born, without stuttering, I will have wild and passionate sex with you until your muscles ache and your eyes water. So, who wants to go first ?'

The Englishman piped up. 'B-b-b-b-b-b-b-irmingham', he said.

'That's no use, Trevor' said the speech therapist, 'Who's next ?'

The Scotsman raised his hand and blurted out 'P-p-p-p-p-p-p-p-aisley'.

'That's no better. There'll be no sex for you, I'm afraid, Hamish. How about you, Paddy?'

The Irishman took a deep breath and eventually blurted out 'London'.

Brilliant, Paddy! said the speech therapist and immediately set about living up to her promise.

After 15 minutes of exceptionally steamy sex, the couple paused for breath and Paddy said

'-d-d-d-d-d-d-d-d-erry'.

JUST PLAIN FUN

A mother was working in the kitchen, listening to her five-year-old son playing with his new electric train set in the living room.

She heard the train stop and her son saying, 'All of You B*****ds who want off, get the f**k off now, cause we're in a hurry! And all of you B*****ds who are getting on, get the f**k on,

The horrified mother went in and told her son, 'We don't Use that kind of language in this house. Now I want you to go to your room and stay there for TWO HOURS. When you come out, you may play with your train, but I want You to Use nice language.'

Two hours later, the son came out of the bedroom and resumed Playing with his train. Soon the train stopped and the mother heard her son say, 'All passengers who are disembarking the train, please remember to take all of your belongings with you. We thank you for travelling with us today and hope your trip was a pleasant one.'

ing, we ask you to stow all of your hand luggage under your seat. Remember, there is no smoking on the train. We hope you will have a pleasant and relaxing journey with us Today.'

As the mother began to smile, the child added ...
'For those of you who are pissed off about the TWO HOUR delay, please see the fat bitch in the kitchen.'

JUST PLAIN FUN

An Irishman named O'Malley

An Irishman named O'Malley went to his doctor after a long illness. The doctor sighed and looked O'Malley in the eye and said, 'I've some bad news for you. You have cancer, and it can't be cured. You'd best put your affairs in order.'

O'Malley was shocked but being a solid character, he managed to compose himself and walk from the doctor's office into the waiting room, where his son was waiting.

'Well, Son,' O'Malley said, 'We Irish celebrate when things are good, and we celebrate when things don't go well. In this case, things aren't so well ... I have cancer. Let's head to the pub and have a few pints.'

After 3 or 4 pints the two were feeling a little less sombre. There were some laughs and some more beers. They were eventually approached by some of O'Malley's friends who were curious as to what the two were celebrating.

O'Malley told them they were drinking to his impending end. He told his friends, 'I have been diagnosed with AIDS.' The friends gave O'Malley their condolences, and they had a couple of more beers. After the friends left, O'Malley's son leaned over and whispered his confusion. 'Dad, I thought you told me that you were dying of cancer ... but you just told your friends that you were dying of AIDS!'

O'Malley said, 'I don't want any of them sleeping with your Mother after I'm gone.'

JUST PLAIN FUN

A young man named Gordon bought a horse from an old farmer for £100.

The farmer agreed to deliver the horse the next day, but when the farmer drove up he said, 'Sorry son, but I have some bad news... the horse is on my truck, but unfortunately he's dead.'

Gordon replied, 'Well then, just give me my money back.'

The farmer said, 'I can't do that, because I've spent it already.'

Gordon said, 'OK then, we'll just unload the horse anyway.' The

farmer asked, 'What are you going to do with him?' Gordon

answered, 'I'm going to raffle him off.' To which the farmer exclaimed, 'Surely you can't raffle off a dead horse!'

But Gordon, with a wicked smile on his face said, 'Of course I can, you watch me. I just won't bother to tell anybody that he's dead.'

A month later the farmer met up with Gordon and asked, 'What happened with that dead horse?'

Gordon said, 'I raffled him off, sold 500 tickets at two pounds a piece, and made a huge, fat profit!!'

Totally amazed, the farmer asked, 'Didn't anyone complain that you had stolen their money because you lied about the horse being dead?'

To which Gordon replied, 'The only guy who found out about the horse being dead was the raffle winner when he came to claim his prize. So I gave him his £2 raffle ticket money back plus an extra £200, which as you know is double the going rate for a horse, so he thought I was a great guy!'

Gordon grew up and eventually became the Chancellor of the Exchequer, and no matter how many times he lied, or how much money he stole from the British voters, as long as he gave them back some of the stolen money, most of them, unfortunately, still thought he was a great guy.

The moral of this story is that, if you think Gordon is about to play fair and do something for the everyday people of the country for once in his miserable, lying life, think again my friend, because you'll be better off flogging a dead horse!

JUST PLAIN FUN

This has got to be one of the cleverest E-mails I've received in a while ...

Someone out there either has too much spare time or is deadly at Scrabble.
(Wait till you see the last one)!

DORMITORY: When you rearrange the letters:
DIRTY ROOM

PRESBYTERIAN: When you rearrange the letters:
BEST IN PRAYER

ASTRONOMER: When you rearrange the letters:
MOON STARER

DESPERATION: When you rearrange the letters:
A ROPE ENDS IT

THE EYES: When you rearrange the letters:
THEY SEE

GEORGE BUSH: When you rearrange the letters:
HE BUGS GORE

THE MORSE CODE: When you rearrange the letters:
HERE COME DOTS

SLOT MACHINES: When you rearrange the letters:
CASH LOST IN ME

JUST PLAIN FUN

ANIMOSITY: When you rearrange the letters:
IS NO AMITY

ELECTION RESULTS: When you rearrange the letters:
LIES - LET'S RECOUNT

SNOOZE ALARMS: When you rearrange the letters:
ALAS! NO MORE Z 'S

A DECIMAL POINT: When you rearrange the letters:
IM A DOT IN PLACE

THE EARTHQUAKES: When you rearrange the letters:
THAT QUEER SHAKE

ELEVEN PLUS TWO: When you rearrange the letters:
TWELVE PLUS ONE

AND FOR THE GRAND FINALE ...

MOTHER-IN-LAW:
When you rearrange the letters:
WOMAN HITLER

JUST PLAIN FUN

Next time you think your hotel bill is too high you might want to consider this ...

A husband and wife are travelling by car from Brisbane to Melbourne.

After almost ten hours on the road, they're too tired to continue and they decide to stop for a rest. They stop at a nice hotel and take a room, but they only plan to sleep for four hours and then get back on the road.

When they check out four hours later, the desk clerk; hands them a bill for $450.00. The man explodes and demands to know why the charge is so high. He tells the clerk although it's a nice hotel; the rooms certainly aren't worth $450.00.

When the clerk tells him $450.00 is the standard rate, the man insists on speaking to the Manager.

The Manager appears, listens to the man, and then explains that the hotel has an Olympic-sized pool and a huge conference centre that were available for the husband and wife to use.

'But we didn't use them,' the man complains.

'Well, they are here, and you could have,' explains the Manager.

JUST PLAIN FUN

He goes on to explain they could have taken in one of the shows for which the hotel is Famous. 'The best entertainers from New York, Hollywood, and LasVegas Perform here,' the Manager says.

'But we didn't go to any of those shows,' complains the man again.

'Well, we have them, and you could have,' the Manager replies.

No matter what amenity the Manager mentions, the man replies, 'But we didn't use it!'

The Manager is unmoved, and eventually the man gives up and agrees to pay. He writes a check and gives it to the Manager.

The Manager is surprised when he looks at the cheque.

'But sir,' he says, 'this cheque is only made out for $50.00.'

'That's correct,' says the man. 'I charged you $400.00 for sleeping with my Wife.'

'But I didn't!' exclaims the Manager.

'Well, too bad,' the man replies. 'She was here and you could have.'

JUST PLAIN FUN

Some guy bought a new fridge for his house. To get rid of his old fridge, he put it in his front yard and hung a sign on it saying: 'Free to good home. You want it, you take it.' For three days the fridge sat there without even one person looking twice at it. He eventually decided that people were too un-trusting of this deal. It looked to good to be true, so he changed the sign to read: 'Fridge for sale $50.' The next day someone stole it.*

One day I was walking down the beach with some friends when someone shouted ... 'Look at that dead bird!' Someone looked up at the sky and said ... 'where?'

While looking at a house, my brother asked the estate agent which direction was north because, he explained, he didn't want the sun waking him up every morning. She asked, 'Does the sun rise in the north?' When my brother explained that the sun rises in the east, and has for some time, she shook her head and said, 'Oh, I don't keep up with that stuff'.

My colleague and I were eating our lunch in our cafeteria, when we overheard one of the administrative assistants talking about the sunburn she got on her weekend drive to the beach. She drove down in a convertible, but 'didn't think she'd get sunburned because the car was moving'.

JUST PLAIN FUN

I told the girl at the steakhouse register that I wanted the half kilogram sirloin. She informed me they only had an 500g sirloin. Not wanting to make a scene, I told her I would take the 500g steak instead of the half-kilogram.

My sister has a lifesaving tool in her car it's designed to cut through a seat belt if she gets trapped She keeps it in the boot.

My friends and I were on a Lager run and noticed that the cases were discounted 10%. Since it was a big party, we bought 2 cases. The cashier multiplied 2 times 10% and gave us a 20% discount.

I was hanging out with a friend when we saw a woman with a nose ring attached to an earring by a chain. My friend said, 'Wouldn't the chain rip out every time she turned her head?' I had to explain that a person's nose and ear remain the same distance apart no matter which way the head is turned.

JUST PLAIN FUN

I couldn't find my luggage at the airport baggage area. So I went to the lost luggage office and told the woman there that my bags never showed up. She smiled and told me not to worry because she was a trained professional and I was in good hands. 'Now,' she asked me, 'Has your plane arrive yet?'

While working at a pizza parlour I observed a man ordering a small pizza to go. He appeared to be alone and the cook asked him if he would like it cut into 4 pieces or 6. He thought about it for some time before responding. 'Just cut it into 4 pieces; I don't think I'm hungry enough to eat 6 pieces.'

Sadly, not only do they walk among us, they also reproduce!

OOPS!

JUST PLAIN FUN

PLEASE, DON'T TALK TO MY PARROT!

Wanda's dishwasher quit working so she called in
a repairman.

Since she had to go to work the next day, she told the
repairman, 'I'll leave the key under the mat. Fix the dishwasher,
leave the bill on the counter, and I'll mail you a cheque.'

'Oh, by the way don't worry about my dog SPIKE.
He won't bother you.'

'But, whatever you do, do NOT, under ANY circumstances,
talk to my parrot!'

JUST PLAIN FUN

'I MUST STRESS TO YOU: DO NOT TALK TO MY PARROT!'

When the repairman arrived at Wanda's apartment the following day, he discovered the biggest, meanest looking dog he has ever seen. But, just as Wanda had said, the dog just lay there on the carpet watching the repairman go about his work.

The parrot, however, drove him nuts the whole time with his incessant yelling, cursing and name calling.

Finally the repairman couldn't contain himself any longer and yelled, 'Shut up, you stupid, ugly bird!'

To which the parrot replied:

'GET HIM SPIKE!'

See ... men just don't listen!

JUST PLAIN FUN

A woman was helping her husband set up his computer, and at the appropriate point in the process, she told him that he would now need to enter a password. Something he could remember easily and will use each time he has to log on.

The husband was in a rather amorous mood and figured he would try for the shock effect to bring this to his wife's attention. So, when the computer asked him to enter his password, he made it plainly obvious to his wife that he was keying in ...

P ...

E ...

N ...

I ...

S ...

His wife fell off her chair laughing when the computer replied:

PASSWORD REJECTED ... NOT LONG ENOUGH

JUST PLAIN FUN

Revenge is sweet

Golf for beginners

Parents can be so cruel

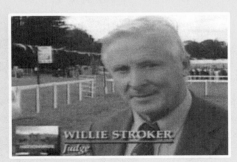

JUST PLAIN FUN

Say it slowly ...

A Kodak Moment

How men screw up romance

JUST PLAIN FUN

Rudolph's first cousin on his mother's side, Shlomo.

JUST PLAIN FUN

Sign over a gynaecologist's Office:

Dr. Jones,
at your cervix

In a Podiatrist's office:

time wounds all heels.

On a Septic Tank Truck:

yesterday's meals on wheels

On a Plumber's truck:

we repair what your
husband fixed

On another Plumber's truck:

don't sleep with a drip.
call your plumber

On a Church's Bill board:

7 days without
God makes one
weak

JUST PLAIN FUN

At a Tyre Store:

invite us to your
next blowout

On an Electrician's truck:

let us remove your shorts

In a Non-smoking Area:

If we see smoke, we will
assume you are on fire and
take appropriate action

On a Maternity Room door:

Push. Push. Push.

At an Optometrist's Office:

if you don't see what you're
looking for, you've come to the
right place

JUST PLAIN FUN

On a Taxidermist's window:

we really know our stuff

On a Fence:

salesmen welcome!
dog food is expensive!

At a Car Dealership:

the best way to get back on
your feet - miss a car payment

Outside a Car Exhaust Store:

no appointment necessary.
we hear you coming

In a Vets waiting room:

be back in 5 minutes.
sit! stay!

JUST PLAIN FUN

In a Restaurant window:

don't stand there and be hungry; come on in and get fed up

In the front yard of a Funeral Home:

drive carefully. we'll wait

And don't forget the sign at a Radiator Shop:

best place in town to
take a leak

Sign on the back of yet another Septic Tank Truck:

caution - this truck is full of
political promises

JUST PLAIN FUN

Stay!

I pulled into the crowded parking lot at the local shopping center and rolled Down the car windows to make sure my Labrador Retriever Pup had fresh air.

She was stretched full-out on the back seat and I wanted to impress upon her that she must remain there.

I walked to the kerb backward, Pointing my finger at the car and saying emphatically, 'Now you stay. Do you hear me? Stay! Stay!'

The driver of a nearby car, a pretty blonde young lady, Gave me a strange look and said, 'Why don't you just put it in Park?'

No Sex since 1957

A crusty old Marine Sergeant Major found himself at a gala event hosted by a local liberal arts college. There was no shortage of extremely young, idealistic ladies in attendance, one of whom approached the Sergeant Major for conversation.

'Excuse me, Sergeant Major, but you seem to be a very serious man. Is something bothering you?'

'Negative, ma'am. Just serious by nature.'

The young lady looked at his awards and decorations on his

JUST PLAIN FUN

uniform and said, 'It looks like you have seen a lot of action.'

'Yes, ma'am, a lot of action. Korea, Vietnam and Iraq'.

The young lady, tiring of trying to start up a conversation, said, 'You know, you should lighten up a little. Relax and enjoy yourself.'

The Sergeant Major just continued to stare at her in his serious manner.

Finally the young lady said, 'You know, I hope you don't take this the wrong way, but when is the last time you had sex?'

'1957, ma'am.'

'Well, there you are. You really need to chill out and quit taking everything so seriously! I mean, no sex since 1957!'

She smiled, winked, and took his hand and led him to a private room where she proceeded to 'relax' him several times ... in several different positions.

Afterwards, panting for breath, she leaned against his bare chest and said, 'Wow, you sure didn't forget much since 1957!'

The Sergeant Major, glancing at his watch, said in his matter-of-fact deadpan voice, 'I hope not, it's only 2130 now.'

JUST PLAIN FUN

Supermarket Greeter:

I had ambitions of finding a simple, uncomplicated part time job after retiring from my 'day job'. Unfortunately, as I have gotten a little older, I have become a little less sensitive. So after landing my new job as a Supermarket greeter, a good find for many retirees, I lasted less than a day ...

About two hours into my first day on the job a very loud, unattractive, mean-acting woman with an estuary accent walked into the store with her two kids, yelling obscenities at them all the way through the entrance.

As I had been instructed, I said pleasantly, 'Good morning, and welcome. Nice children you have there. Are they twins?'

The ugly woman stopped yelling long enough to say, 'Hell no, they ain't twins. The oldest one's 9, and the other one's 7. Why the hell would you think they're twins? Are you blind, or just stupid?'

So I replied, 'I'm neither blind nor stupid, Ma'am, I just couldn't believe you got fu**ed twice. Have a good day and thank you for shopping with us.'

My supervisor said I probably wasn't cut out for this line of work ...

JUST PLAIN FUN

Israel - Jerusalem:
Wailing Wall / Western Wall

A female CNN journalist heard about a very old Jewish man who had been going to the Western Wall to pray, twice a day, every day, for a long, long time. So she went to check it out as a possible human interest story.

She approached the Western Wall and there she happened upon the old Jewish man who was walking slowly up to the holy site.

She watched the old Jew pray. Then, after about 45 minutes, the old Jew – using a cane and moving very slowly – turned to leave The Wall. Respectfully, the CNN Reporter approached the old Jew for an interview.

JUST PLAIN FUN

'Pardon me, sir, I'm Rebecca Smith from CNN. What's your name?'

'Morris Fishbien', he replied.

'Sir, how long have you been coming to the Western Wall and praying?'

'For about 60 years'.

'60 years! That's amazing! What do you pray for?'

'I pray for peace between the Christians, Jews and the Muslims. I pray for all the wars and all the hatred to stop. I pray for all our children to grow up safely as responsible adults, and to respect their parents and to love and be charitable to their fellow man.'

'So, how do you feel after doing this for 60 years?'

'I feel Like I'm talking to a fu*king brick wall!'

JUST PLAIN FUN

Prince Charles is visiting a hospital in Glasgow and is being introduced to some patients.

He asks the first how he is doing and the patient replies:
'Fair fa' your honest sonsie face,
Great chieftain of the puddin' race,'

He moves on to another who responds to Charles's enquiry thus:
'And surely ye'll be your pint-stowp,
And surely I'll be mine,
And we'll take a cup of kindness yet,
For auld lang syne!'

Charles is ushered by a nurse to a third patient and asks how he is doing and the patient says:
'O my luve is like a red, red rose,
That's newly sprung in June,
O my luve is like a melodie,
That's sweetly play'd in June.'

Charles turns to the nurse and says 'Clearly this must be the mental ward'.

'No', the nurse says, 'It's the Serious <u>Burns</u> Unit'

JUST PLAIN FUN

Testicle Therapy

Two women were playing golf, one teed off and watched in horror as her ball headed directly toward a foursome of men playing the next hole.

The ball hit one of the men.

He immediately clasped his hands together at his groin, fell to the ground and proceeded to roll around in agony.

The woman rushed down to the man, and immediately began to apologize. 'Please allow me to help. I'm a Physical Therapist and I know I could relieve your pain if you'd allow me,' she told him.

'Oh, no, I'll be all right. I'll be fine in a few minutes,' the man replied. He was in obvious agony, lying in the fetal position, still clasping his hands there at his groin.

At her persistence, however, he finally allowed her to help.

She gently took his hands away and laid them to the side, loosened his pants and put her hands inside.

She administered tender and artful massage for several long moments and asked, 'How does that feel?'

He replied: 'It feels great, but I still think my thumb's broken!'

JUST PLAIN FUN

Snow Scam

I believe this scam is spreading across England, so thought you should be warned.

Heavy falls of snow are forecast and I wanted to warn you of this scam. Please be on the lookout for this pair in case they appear at your door.

They offered to shovel the snow from my driveway for only £10. Not ten minutes into the job they were at my door complaining about being cold. They said they wanted to come in to my house and get warm for a while.

Well, three hours later, they ended up leaving without finishing the driveway. I didn't get anything done around the house because I was afraid to take my eyes off of them.

Please don't let this happen to you!

Fortunately, I took their picture before they left so you should be able to identify them if they call on you. If these two appear on your doorstep, don't say you weren't warned!

JUST PLAIN FUN

I'm sending this to you as you are just the sort of person to be taken in by these rogues!

JUST PLAIN FUN

Bridge In France

Over the past few years I have received many emails showing things that are funny but rather superficial and I have been guilty of forwarding them on to my friends, like you.

Sometimes I even send pictures of naked women, which is in bad taste for (some of) my friends, but I have seen the light.

From now on I am only sending you pictures from old monuments, nature and other cultural sights which are healthy and educational for your mind.

Below is a picture of the bridge 'Pont Neuf' (Bridge Nine) in Toulouse, France. It's a priceless 14th century landmark.

Isn't it absolutely beautiful?

JUST PLAIN FUN

The following squads have just been announced for the 2010 World Cup

BRAZILIAN SQUAD FOR WORLD CUP 2010

Pinnochio
Libero
Vimto Memento Borneo Tango
Cheerio Subbuteo
Scenario Fellatio
Portfolio
SUBS:
Placebo
Porno
Polio
Banjo
Brasso
Stereo (L)
Stereo (R)
Hydrochlorofluoro
Aristotle
Computersezno

YUGOSLAVIAN SQUAD FOR WORLD CUP 2010

Itch
Annoyingitch, Hardtoreachitch, Scratchanitch
Hic Sic Spic Pric
Digaditch, Fallinaditch
Horseraditch
SUBS:
Mowapitch
Letsgetrich
Shagabitch

JUST PLAIN FUN

RUSSIAN SQUAD FOR WORLD CUP 2010
Whodyanicabolicov
Ticlycov, Chesticov, Nasticov
Slalomsky, Downhillsky
Risky, Swedishshev, Mastershev
Fuckov, Ufuckov
SUBS:
Rubitov
Gechakitov
Sodov
Pastryshev
Najinsky
Ivorripabollockov
Taykitov

ROMANIAN SQUAD FOR WORLD CUP 2010
Chatanoogaciouciou
Atishiou, Blessiou, Thankyiou
Busqueue, Snookercu
Pennyciou, Twoapennyciou, Fourapennyciou
I'llgetciou, Youandwhosarmi
SUBS:
U
NonU
ManU
Stuffyiou
Lee Kwan Yu

DANISH SQUAD FOR WORLD CUP 2010
Toomanigoalssen
Tryandstopussen, Crapdefenssen, Haveagossen
Firstsson, Seccondsson

JUST PLAIN FUN

Thirdsson
Legshurtssen, Notroubleseeingussen
Wherestheballssen, Getthebeerssen
SUBS:
Howmanygoalsisthatssen
Finallygaveupcountinssen
Hurryupandblowthewhistlessen
Yourelatedtoalexfergusonssen

ITALIAN SQUAD FOR WORLD CUP 2010

Baloni
Potabelli, Beerabelli, Giveitsumwelli
Wotsontelli, Yrarseissmelli, Onetoomani
Legslikejelli, Havabenni
Wobblijelli, Spendapenni
SUBS:
Cantthinkofani!!!
Buggermi

MEXICAN SQUAD FOR WORLD CUP 2010

San Francisco
Costa Brava, Hopelez Juan Andonly
Manuel Gearbox
Don Criformi-Argentina, Skrewdigalz Luis Canon Sombrero
Chihuahua Jose
SUBS:
Jesus Maria Don Key
Burrito
Speedy Gonzalez
Tequila
Caramba

JUST PLAIN FUN

DUTCH SQUAD FOR WORLD CUP 2010

Kenning van Hire
Van Diemansland, Van der Valk, Van Gard, Van Erealdizeez
Ad van Tagus, Hertz van Rental, Transit van Dors
Van Coova, Van Sprokendown, Aye van Hoe
SUBS:
Van Iller
Van Ishincreme
Van Morrison

Two players who are not included are Russian hard-man
Sendimov, who will be serving a three-month suspension, and
the hard-working Mexican midfielder, Manuel Labor.
There is no place in the Dutch squad for lesbian tranny, Dick
van Dyke.
The young Dutch star Per Vert has been excluded from the
squad, after he was discovered in the back streets of
Amsterdam with his finger in a dyke.

EDUCATION

Gordon Brown was visiting a primary school and he visited one of the classes. They were in the middle of a discussion related to words and their meanings. The teacher asked Mr Brown if he would like to lead the discussion on the word 'tragedy'. Thus the illustrious leader asked the class for an example of a tragedy.

A little boy stood up and offered: 'If my best friend, who lives on a farm, is playing in the field and a tractor runs over him and kills him that would be a tragedy.'

'No', said Gordon, 'that would be an accident.'

A little girl raised her hand: 'If a school bus carrying fifty children drove over a cliff, killing everyone inside, that would be a tragedy'.

'I'm afraid not', explained Gordon - 'that's what we would call great loss'

The room went silent. No other children volunteered. Gordon searched the room. 'Isn't there anyone here who can give me an example of a tragedy?'

Finally, at the back of the room, little Jeremy raised his hand. In a quiet voice he said: 'If a plane carrying you and Mr Darling to Afghanistan or Iraq was struck by a 'friendly fire' missile and blown to smithereens, that would be a tragedy.'

EDUCATION

'Fantastic!' exclaimed Gordon. 'That's right. And can you tell me why that would be tragedy?'

'Well,' says little Jeremy 'it has to be a tragedy, because it certainly wouldn't be a great loss and it probably wouldn't be a f*cking accident either!'

EDUCATION

Today Kids Are Quick To Respond or just plain Cheeky.

TEACHER: Maria, go to the map and find North America.
MARIA: Here it is.
TEACHER: Correct. Now class, who discovered America?
CLASS: Maria.

:)

TEACHER: John, why are you doing your math multiplication on the floor?
JOHN: You told me to do it without using tables.

:)

TEACHER: Glenn, how do you spell 'crocodile?'
GLENN: K-R-O-K-O-D-I-A-L
TEACHER: No, that's wrong
GLENN: Maybe it is wrong, but you asked me how I spell it.

:)

TEACHER: Donald, what is the chemical formula for water?
DONALD: H I J K L M N O.
TEACHER: What are you talking about?
DONALD: Yesterday you said it's H to O.

:)

TEACHER: Winnie, name one important thing we have today that we didn't have ten years ago.
WINNIE: Me!

EDUCATION

TEACHER: Glen, why do you always get so dirty?
GLEN: Well, I'm a lot closer to the ground than you are.

TEACHER: Millie, give me a sentence starting with 'I.'
MILLIE: I is ...
TEACHER: No Millie, always say, 'I am.'
MILLIE: All right, I am the ninth letter of the alphabet.

TEACHER: George Washington not only chopped down his father's cherry tree, but also admitted it. Now, Louie, do you know why his father didn't punish him?
LOUIS: Because George still had the axe in his hand.

TEACHER: Now, Simon, tell me frankly, do you say prayers before eating?
SIMON: No sir, I don't have to, my Mom is a good cook.

TEACHER: Clyde, your composition on 'My Dog' is exactly the same as your brother's. Did you copy his?
CLYDE :   No, sir. It's the same dog.

TEACHER: Harold, what do you call a person who keeps on talking when people are no longer interested?
HAROLD: A teacher

EDUCATION

What Makes 100%?

What does it mean to give MORE than 100%?

Ever wonder about those people who say they are giving more than 100%?

We have all been to those meetings where someone wants you to give over 100%.

How about achieving 103%?

What makes up 100% in life?

Here's a little mathematical formula that might help you answer these questions:

If:
A B C D E F G H I J K L M N O P Q R S T U V W X Y Z
is represented as:
1 2 3 4 5 6 7 8 9 10 11 12 13 14 15 16 17 18 19 20 21 22 23 24 25 26.
Then:
H-A -R -D-W-O -R -K
$8+1+18+4+23+15+18+11 = 98\%$
and
K -N -O -W-L -E-D-G-E
$11+14+15+23+12+5+4+7+5 = 96\%$

143

EDUCATION

But
A-T -T -I -T -U -D-E
1+20+20+9+20+21+4+5 = 100%
And,
B -U -L -L -S -H-I -T
2+21+12+12+19+8+9+20 = 103%
AND, look how far ass kissing will take you.
A-S -S -K -I -S-S -I -N-G
1+19+19+11+9+19+19+9+14+7 = 118%

So, one can conclude with mathematical certainty, that While Hard work and Knowledge will get you close, and Attitude will get you there, it's the Bullshit and Ass kissing that will put you over the top.

'REMEMBER SOME PEOPLE ARE ALIVE SIMPLY BECAUSE IT IS ILLEGAL TO SHOOT THEM'

EDUCATION

CREATIVE PUNS FOR 'EDUCATED MINDS'

🙂 The roundest knight at King Arthur's round table was Sir Cumference. He acquired his size from too much pi.

🙂 I thought I saw an eye doctor on an Alaskan island, but it turned out to be an optical Aleutian.

🙂 She was only a whisky maker, but he loved her still.

🙂 A rubber band pistol was confiscated from algebra class because it was a weapon of math disruption.

🙂 The butcher backed into the meat grinder and got a little behind in his work.

🙂 No matter how much you push the envelope, it'll still be stationery.

🙂 A dog gave birth to puppies near the road and was cited for littering.

🙂 A grenade thrown into a kitchen in France would result in Linoleum Blownapart.
Two silk worms had a race. They ended up in a tie.

🙂 Time flies like an arrow. Fruit flies like a banana.
A hole has been found in the nudist camp Wall. The police are looking into it.

🙂 Atheism is a non-prophet organization.

EDUCATION

Two hats were hanging on a hat rack in the hallway. One hat said to the other, 'You stay here; I'll go on a head.'

I wondered why the baseball kept getting bigger. Then it hit me.

A sign on the lawn at a drug rehab center said: 'Keep off the Grass.'

A small boy swallowed some coins and was taken to a hospital. When his grandmother telephoned to ask how he was, a nurse said, 'No change yet.'

A chicken crossing the road is poultry in motion.

The short fortune-teller who escaped from prison was a small medium at large.

The man who survived mustard gas and pepper spray is now a seasoned veteran.

A backward poet writes inverse.

In democracy it's your vote that counts. In feudalism it's your count that votes.

When cannibals ate a missionary, they got a taste of religion.

Don't join dangerous cults: Practice Safe sects!

EDUCATION

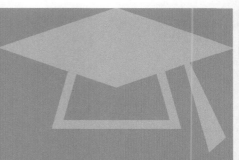

Knowing how **fond you are of the written** word and

correct pronunciation ...

I though you should be aware of this.

There is a right way and a wrong way to pronounce

Oklahoma

The proper way is:

OKLA ... HOMA

There's a pause between the 'a' and the 'h'
- I can prove it ...

EDUCATION

There, you learned something today!

I do love these educational E Mails ... Don't you?

EDUCATION

The Pakistani Boarder

A grade three teacher is giving a lesson on nutrition, and she decides to ask her students? what they had for breakfast. To add a spelling component, she asks the students to also spell their answers.

Susan puts up her hand and says she had an egg, 'E-G-G'. 'Very good', says the teacher.

Peter says he had toast. 'T-O-A-S-T'.
'Excellent.'

Johnny has his hand up and the teacher reluctantly calls on him. 'I had Bugger all', he says, 'B-U-G-G-E-R-A-L-L'. The teacher is mortified and scolds Johnny for his rude answer.

Later when the lesson turns to geography, she asks the students some rudimentary questions.

Susan correctly identifies the Capital of Canada Peter is able to tell her which ocean is off Canada's east coast. When it's Johnny's turn, the teacher remembers his rude answer from the nutrition lesson, and decides to give him a very difficult question. 'Johnny', she asks, 'Where is the Pakistani border?'

Johnny ponders the question and finally says, 'The Pakistani boarder is in bed with my mother. That's why I got Bugger all for breakfast'.

EDUCATION

Many Syrians struggle to even read Arabic, much less have a clue about reading English.

So, how do a group of Syrian protest leaders create the most impact with their signs by having the standard 'Death To Americans'(etc.) slogans printed in English?

Answer:

They simply hire an English-speaking civilian to translate and write their statements into English.

Unfortunately, in this case, they were unaware that the 'civilian' insurance company employee hired for the job was a retired US Army Sergeant! Obviously, the results were PRICELESS!

This picture is not doc-tored.

EDUCATION

LITTLE HARRY ON MATHS (Part 1)

A teacher asks her class, 'If there are 5 birds sitting on a fence, and you shoot one of them, how many will be left?' She calls on little Harry.
He replies, 'None, they will all fly away with the first gunshot.'
The teacher replies, 'The correct answer is 4, but I like your thinking.'
Then little Harry says, 'I have a question for YOU Miss Rogers ...
There are 3 women sitting on a bench having ice cream:
One is delicately licking the sides of the triple scoop of ice cream.
The second is gobbling down the top and sucking on the cone.
The third is biting off the top of the ice cream.
Which one is married?'
The teacher, blushing a great deal, replied, 'Well, I suppose the one that's gobbled down the top and sucked the cone.'
To which Little Harry replies, 'The correct answer is the one with the wedding-ring on ... but I like your thinking.'

LITTLE HARRY ON MATHS (Part 2)

Little Harry returns from school and says he got an 'F' in arithmetic.
'Why'?' asks the father.
'The teacher asked "How much is 2 x 3", so I said 6', replies Harry.
'But that's right' says his father.
'Yeah, but then she asked me, "How much is 3 x 2"'
'What's the fuckin' difference?' asks the father.
'That's what I said' replied Harry.

EDUCATION

LITTLE HARRY ON ENGLISH

Little Harry goes to school, and the teacher says, 'Today we aregoing to learn multi-syllable words in our class. Does anybody have an example of a multi-syllable word?'
Harry says 'Mas-tur-bate.'
Miss Rogers smiles and says, 'Wow, Harry, that's a real mouthful.'
Little Harry says, 'No, Miss Rogers, you're thinking of a blow-job.'

LITTLE HARRY ON GRAMMAR (Part 1)
Little Harry was sitting in the class one day. All of a sudden, he needed to go to the bathroom. He yelled out, 'Miss Jones, I need to go take a piss!!'
The teacher replied, 'Now Harry, that is NOT the proper word to use in this situation. The correct word you want to is, "I need to Urinate" Please use the word 'ur-i-nate' in a sentence correctly,and I will allow you to go.'
Little Harry thinks for a bit, and then says, 'YOUR'E AN EIGHT, but if you had bigger tits, you'd be a TEN'

LITTLE HARRY ON GRAMMAR (Part 2)
One day, during lessons on proper grammar, the teacher asked for a show of hands from those who could use the word 'beautiful' in the same sentence twice.
First, she called on little Suzie, who responded with, 'My father bought my mother a beautiful dress, and she looked beautiful in it.'
'Very good, Suzie,' replied the teacher.
She then called on little Michael.

EDUCATION

'My mommy planned a beautiful banquet, and it turned out beauti-
fully.'
She said, 'Excellent, Michael, excellent.'
Then the teacher reluctantly called on little Harry.
'Last night at the dinner table, my sister told my father that she
was pregnant, and he said 'Beautiful, just fuckin' beautiful'.

LITTLE HARRY ON GETTING OLDER

Little Harry was sitting on a park bench, munching on one
candy bar after another.
After the 6th bar, a man on the bench across from him said,
'Son, you know eating all that candy isn't good for you. It will give
you acne, rot your teeth, and make you fat.'
Little Harry replied, 'My grandfather lived to be 107 years old.'
The man asked, 'Did your grandfather eat 6 candy bars at a time'?
Little Harry answered, 'No, he just minded his own f*ckin' busi-
ness.

I LOVE LITTLE HARRY!

Medical Matters

GOVERNMENT HEALTH WARNING

DO NOT SWALLOW CHEWING-GUM !!

Medical Matters

MEDICAL RESEARCH

There is more money being spent on breast implants and Viagra today than on Alzheimer's research.

This means that by 2040, there should be a large elderly population with perky boobs and huge erections and absolutely no recollection of what to do with them!

If you don't send this to five OLD friends (if you can remember their names) there will be five fewer people laughing in the world

Medical Matters

The Swine Flew

Medical Matters

THE LOVE STORY OF RALPH AND EDNA ...

Just because someone doesn't love you the way you want them to, doesn't mean they don't love you with all they have.

Ralph and Edna were both patients in a mental Hospital. One day while they were walking past the hospital swimming pool. Ralph suddenly jumped into the deep end. He sank to the bottom of the pool and stayed there. Edna promptly jumped in to save him. She swam to the bottom and pulled him out. When the Head Nurse, Director became aware of Edna's heroic act she immediately ordered her to be discharged from the hospital, as she now considered her to be mentally stable.

When she went to tell Edna the news she said, 'Edna, I have good news and bad news. The good news is you're being discharged, since you were able to rationally respond to a crisis by jumping in and saving the life of the person you love. I have concluded that your act displays sound mindedness. The bad news is, Ralph hung himself in the bathroom with his bathrobe belt right after you saved him. I am so sorry, but he's dead.'

Edna replied, 'He didn't hang himself, I put him there to dry. How soon can I go home?'

Happy Mental Health Day!
You can do your bit by remembering to send an email to an unstable friend ...

Done my part!

Medical Matters

DOCTOR VISIT - THIS IS BRILLIANT!

There's nothing worse than a receptionist who insists you tell her what is wrong with you in a room full of other patients. Many of us have experienced this, and I love the way this old guy handled it.

An 86-year-old man walked into a crowded waiting room and approached the desk. The receptionist said, 'hello, sir. Can you please tell me why you're here to see the doctor today?'

'There's something wrong with my dick,' he replied.

The receptionist became irritated and said, 'you shouldn't come into a crowded waiting room and say things like that.'

'Why not? You asked me what was wrong and I told you,' he said.

The receptionist replied, 'now you've caused some embarrassment in this room full of people. You should have said there is something wrong with your ear or something and discussed the problem further with the doctor in private.'

The man replied, 'you shouldn't ask people questions in a room full of strangers, if the answer could embarrass anyone.' The man walked out, waited several minutes and then re-entered.

The receptionist smiled smugly and asked, 'Yes?'

'There's something wrong with my ear,' he stated.

Medical Matters

The receptionist nodded approvingly and smiled, knowing he had taken her advice. 'And what is wrong with your ear, sir?'

'I can't piss out of it,' he replied.

The waiting room erupted in laughter.

A man goes to an oral surgeon to have a tooth pulled. The Dentist pulls out a freezing needle to give the man a shot. 'No way! No needles! I hate needles,' the patient said.

The Dentist starts to hook up the laughing gas and the man objects. 'I can't do the gas thing. The thought of having the gas mask on is suffocating me!'

The Dentist then asks the patient if he has any objection to taking a pill. 'No objection,' the patient says. 'I'm fine with pills.'

The Dentist then returns and says, 'Here's a Viagra tablet.'

The patient says, 'Wow! I didn't know Viagra worked as a pain killer!'

It doesn't,' said the Dentist, 'but it will give you something to hold on to when I pull your tooth'.

Medical Matters

BLACK TESTICLES

A male patient is lying in bed in the hospital, wearing an oxygen mask over his mouth and nose, still heavily sedated from a difficult four hour surgical procedure.

A young student nurse appears to give him a partial sponge bath. 'Nurse,' he mumbles, from behind the mask 'Are my testicles black?'

Embarrassed, the young nurse replies 'I don't know, Sir. I'm only here to wash your upper body.'

He struggles to ask again, 'Nurse, are my testicles black?'

Concerned that he may elevate his vitals from worry about his testicles, she overcomes her embarrassment and sheepishly pulls back the covers.

She raises his gown, holds his penis in one hand and his testicles in the other, lifting and moving them around and around gently.

Then, she takes a close look and says, 'No sir, they aren't and I assure you, there's nothing wrong with them, Sir!'

The man pulls off his oxygen mask, smiles at her and says very slowly, 'Thank you very much. That was wonderful, but listen very, very closely ... A r e - m y - t e s t - r e s u l t s - b a c k ? '

DOCTORS RECEPTIONIST BREAKS RECORD WITH ZERO APPOINTMENTS.

Moira Braithwaite, 52, of Dorking, was this morning celebrating her ninth successive Receptionist of the Month award after preventing over 35,000 patients getting an appointment within 48 hours during the month of September alone.

Moira's name will appear in the next Guinness Book of Records as the most effective doctor's receptionist of all time, having not allowed a single appointment to be made with any doctor, despite the desperate pleas of the sick and injured.

Moira uses a number of techniques to prevent patients from seeing their local G.P. 'Sometimes when people ring up she pretends to be a mini-cab company in Bromsgrove and claims that the taxi is on its way. Another time she diverted her number so that people calling the doctors went straight through to the Samaritans.

Although patients are supposed to be able to get an appointment with 48 hours, Moira claims that this figure is intended to represent 48 working hours and anybody stopping work during that time goes to the back of the queue again. She also maintains the right to prevent anybody who may be unwell from visiting the doctor's surgery 'at the risk of them bringing germs into the surgery.' The waiting list for expectant mothers is a year and a half.

The actual surgery has been fitted with a high security door

Medical Matters

leaving visitors to speak into a distorted and inaudible inter-com outside, which allows Moira to pretend that she can't hear them. 'The speaker button also delivers a mild electric shock, which is always an extra deterrent for anyone with a heart condi-tion,' claimed one elderly stroke victim If patients do manage to get inside the next set of doors have no handles and can-not be opened from the outside. Or indeed, from the inside as they are only painted onto the wall.

Moira has also managed to keep mothers away by claiming that 'The normal children's doctor is off sick today but I can make you an appointment with our temporary paediatrician, Dr Glitter.'

Moira was telephoned this morning to ask when she would like to collect her prestigious award, but she claimed that she couldn't offer any slots this week, but we could try ringing back at one second past eight on Monday morning and 'see if we had anything then'. Or we could queue outside the surgery on the off-chance over the weekend, even though it would in fact be closed. And relocated to a secret address in Canada.

Medical Matters

CARDIOVASCULAR HEALTH - SIMPLE EXERCISE

The older we get the more important it is to incorporate exercise into our daily routine. This is necessary to maintain cardiovascular health and maintain muscle mass.

If you're over 40, you might want to take it easy at first, then do more repetitions as you become more proficient and build stamina.

Warning: It may be too strenuous for some. Always consult your doctor before starting any exercise program!

SCROLL DOWN ...

NOW SCROLL UP ...

That's enough for the first day. Great job!

Have a glass of wine.

THE BATHTUB TEST

During a visit to the mental asylum, a visitor asked the Director how do you determine whether or not a patient should be institutionalised.

'Well,' said the Director, 'we fill up a bathtub, then we offer a teaspoon, a teacup and a bucket to the patient and ask him or her to empty the bathtub.'

'Oh, I understand,' said the visitor. 'A normal person would use the bucket because it's bigger than the spoon or the teacup.'

'No' said the Director, 'A normal person would pull the plug out.'

'Do you want a bed near the window?'

THE BEST HOSPITAL SIGN EVER?

Medical Matters

The phone rings and the lady of the house answers, 'Hello Mrs. Sanders, please.'

'Speaking.'

'Mrs. Sanders, this is Doctor Jones at Saint Agnes Laboratory. When your husband's doctor sent his biopsy to the lab last week, a biopsy from another Mr Sanders arrived as well. We are now uncertain which one belongs to your husband. Frankly, either way the results are not too good.'

'What do you mean?' Mrs. Sanders asks nervously.

'Well, one of the specimens tested positive for Alzheimer's and the other one tested positive for HIV. We can't tell which is which.'

'That's dreadful! Can you do the test again?' questioned Mrs. Sanders

'Normally we can, but Medicare will only pay for these expensive tests one time.'

'Well, what am I supposed to do now?'

'The folks at Medicare recommend that you drop your husband off somewhere in the middle of town. If he finds his way home, don't sleep with him.'

Medical Matters

PHARMACOLOGY:

All drugs have two names - a trade name and a generic name. E.g. the trade name of Panadol also has a generic name of Paracetamol. Amoxil is also called Amoxicillin and Nurofen is also called Ibuprofen.

The FDA has been looking for a generic name for Viagra. After careful consideration it recently announced that it has settled on the generic name of ... mycoxafloppin.

Also considered were:

Mycoxafailin,

Mydixadrupin,

Mydixarizin,

Dixafix, and of course,

Ibepokin.

It was announced today that Viagra will soon be available in liquid form, and will be marketed by a Cola company as a power beverage suitable for use as a mixer. It will now be possible for a man to literally pour himself a stiff one. Obviously we can no longer call this a soft drink, and it gives new meaning to the names of 'cocktails', 'highballs' and just a good old-fashioned 'stiff drink'.

Medical Matters

THOUGHT FOR THE DAY:

There is more money being spent on breast implants and Viagra today than on Alzheimer's research.

This means that by 2040, there should be a large elderly population with perky boobs and huge erections and absolutely no recollection of what to do with them.

SWINE FLU WARNING:

If you wake up looking like this, don't go to work.

Medical Matters

SWINE FLU UPDATE

- I called the Swine Flu hotline ... all I got was crackling

- I heard that the first symptom is that you come out in rashers.

- Another is that you get the trotts.

- But, I woke up with pig tails this morning ... Should I be worried?

- The doctor asked me how long I'd had the symptoms of Swine Flu. I said it must have been about a Weeeeeeeeeeeek!

- Apparently my mate's got Swine Flu - I think he's just telling porkies, though.

- The only known cure for Swine Flu in humans has been found to be the liberal application of oinkment.

- I hear there's now a sine flu as well. Someone on the news was going off on a tangent about it.

Medical Matters

- This little piggy went to market,
  This little piggy stayed at home,
  This little piggy had roast beef,
  This little piggy had none.
  And this little piggy had influenza A virus subtype
  hemagglutinin protein 1 neuraminidase protein 1

- Swine flu, however, is not a problem for the pigs because
  they're all going to be cured anyway.

- News Flash ... this is just in. The world's religious leaders
  have issued a joint declaration that the Swine Flu pandemic
  is the start of the aporkalypse.

- I just heard on the news that, 'Swine Flu could potentially
  be a threat to every single person in the world'. Well it's a
  good thing I'm married then, isn't it?

- This is not a time for panic. It is no pig deal. It is a mild
  hamademic, don't believe the spam you're getting.

- Swine flu has now mixed with bird flu. Scientists say they
  will find a cure when pigs fly.

Good Advice

PLEASE READ THE IMPORTANT NOTICE BELOW.

Supermarket car park scam – PLEASE BE AWARE

A warning for you and any of your friends who may be regular supermarket shoppers

Over the last month I became the victim of a clever scam while out shopping. Simply going out to get some shopping turned out to be quite traumatic. Don't be naïve enough to think it couldn't happen to you. Here's how the scam works:

Two seriously good looking 21 year old girls come over to your car as you are loading your groceries into the boot. They both start wiping your windshield with a rag and glass cleaner, with their cleavage almost falling out of their skimpy T-shirts. It is impossible not to look. When you thank them and offer them a tip, they say 'No' and instead ask you for a lift to another shopping centre. You agree and they get into the back seat. On the way they start having sex with each other. Then one of them climbs over into the front seat and performs oral sex on you, while the other one steals your wallet.

I had my wallet stolen on May 4th, 9th, 10th and twice on the 15th, 17th, 20th, June 2nd and 4th, three times on the 5th, three times just yesterday, and very likely again this coming weekend as soon as I can buy more wallets.

YOU HAVE BEEN WARNED!

Good Advice

Tough Love v Spanking
– Good Argument

Most people think it improper to spank children, so I have tried other methods to control my kids when they have one of 'those moments.'

One that I found effective is for me to just take the child for a car ride and talk.

Some say it's the vibration from the car, others say it's the time away from any distractions such as TV, Video Games, Computer, IPod, etc.

Either way, my kids usually calm down and stop misbehaving after our car ride together.

Eye to eye contact helps a lot too.

I've included a photo below of one of my sessions with my grandson, in case you would like to use the technique ...

Good Advice

This works with grandchildren, nieces, and nephews as well.

Dear friends,

I just read an article on the dangers of heavy drinking ...

Scared the shit out of me.

So that's it!

After today, no more reading.

Good Advice

This is exactly why you should always, ALWAYS...
twirl once in front of the mirror before leaving the house.

But just think how many people she made smile
throughout the day!

Good Advice

Why parents should always check their children's homework before they hand it in:

A first grade girl handed in the drawing below for a homework assignment.

After it was graded and the child brought it home, she returned to school the next day with the following note:

Dear Ms. Davis,

I want to be very clear on my child's illustration. It is NOT of me on a dance pole on a stage in a strip joint. I work at Home Depot and had commented to my daughter how much money we made in the recent snowstorm. This picture is of me selling a shovel.

Mrs. Harrington

Good Advice

Please check your kids bags ...

Little Susie goes home from school and tells her mum that the boys keep asking her to do cartwheels because she's very good at them.

Mum said 'You should say 'NO!' - they only want to look at your knickers'

Susie said 'I know they do, that's why I hide them in my bag!'

Good Advice

WHY MEN DON'T WRITE ADVICE COLUMNS

Dear Walter,

I hope you can help me here. The other day, I set off for work leaving my husband in the house watching the TV as usual. I hadn't driven more than a mile down the road when the engine conked out and the car shuddered to a halt. I walked back home to get my husband's help.

When I got home I couldn't believe my eyes. He was in our bedroom with the neighbours' daughter. I'm 32, my husband is 34, and the neighbours' daughter is 22.

We have been married for ten years. When I confronted him, he broke down and admitted that they had been having an affair for the past six months. I told him to stop or I'd leave him. He was let go from his job six months ago and he says he has been feeling increasingly depressed and worthless. I love him very much, but ever since I gave him the ultimatum he has become increasingly distant.

He won't go to counselling and I'm afraid I can't get through to him anymore.

Can you please help?

Sincerely,
Sheila

Good Advice

Dear Sheila:

A car stalling after being driven a short distance can be caused by a variety of faults with the engine... Start by checking that there is no debris in the fuel line. If it's clear, check the vacuum pipes and hoses on the intake manifold and also check all grounding wires. If none of these approaches solves the problem, it could be that the fuel pump itself is faulty, causing low delivery pressure to the injectors.

I hope this helps,

WALTER

Financial and Political

THIS IS SERIOUS STUFF
- FOR CAPITALISTS ...

Following the problems in the sub-prime lending market in America and the run on banks in the UK, uncertainty has now hit Japan.

IN THE LAST 7 DAYS:

Origami Bank has folded

Sumo Bank has gone belly up

Bonsai Bank announced plans to cut some of its branches

Karaoke Bank is up for sale and will likely go for a song

Shares in Kamikaze Bank were suspended after they nose-dived

500 staff at Karate Bank got the chop, and analysts report that there is something fishy going on at Sushi Bank where it is feared that clients and staff may get a raw deal.

Financial and Political

THE FUNERAL

Maurice died, and his will provided £50,000 for an elaborate funeral.

As the last attendees left, Maurice's wife Rose turned to her oldest friend Sadie and said, 'Well, I'm sure Maurice would be well pleased.'

'I'm sure you're right,' replied Sadie, who then leaned in closer to her friend and lowered her voice to a whisper. 'Tell me Rose, how much did the funeral really cost?'

'All of it,' said Rose. 'The whole Fifty thousand.'

'No!' Sadie exclaimed. 'I mean, it was very nice, but really ... £50,000?'

Rose nodded. 'The funeral was £6,500. I donated £500. to the shul for the Rabbi's services. The Shiva food and drinks were another £500. The rest went for the memorial stone.'

Sadie computed quickly. '£42,500 for a memorial stone? Oy vey, how big is it?'

'Ten and a half carats.' she replied

Financial and Political

Dan was single and living at home with his father while working in the family business.

When he learned that he would one day inherit his sickly father's fortune, he decided he needed a wife.

One evening, at an investment seminar, he saw the woman of his dreams! ? She took his breath away. 'I may look ordinary,' he told her, 'but in a few years my father will die and I'll inherit 50 million.'

FINANCIAL PLANNING
LONG TERM: THE CAR IS CHEAPER

Impressed, she accepted his business card and three weeks later she became his stepmother.

Financial and Political

1929 AND NOW ...

Back in the 1929 Financial Crash, it was said that some Wall Street stockbrokers and bankers JUMPED from their office windows and committed suicide when confronted with the news of their firms' and clients' financial ruin.

Many people were said to almost feel a little sorry for them.

In 2010 the attitude has changed somewhat ...

Financial and Political

SUBJECT: TWO COWS

You have two cows ...

SOCIALISM:
You have 2 cows.
You give one to your neighbour.

COMMUNISM:
You have 2 cows.
The State takes both and gives you some milk.

FASCISM:
You have 2 cows.
The State takes both and sells you some milk.

NAZISM:
You have 2 cows.
The State takes both and shoots you.

BUREAUCRACY:
You have 2 cows.
The State takes both, shoots one, milks the other, then throws the milk away due to possible risk of lead contamination from the shooting.

SURREALISM:
You have two giraffes.
The government requires you to take harmonica lessons.

Financial and Political

TRADITIONAL CAPITALISM:
You have two cows.
You sell one and buy a bull. Your herd multiplies, and the economy grows.
You sell them and retire on the income.

AN AMERICAN CORPORATION:
You have two cows.
You sell one, and force the other to produce the milk of four cows.
Later, you hire a consultant to analyse why the cow has dropped dead.

A FRENCH CORPORATION:
You have two cows.
You go on strike, organise a riot, and block the roads, because you want three cows.

A JAPANESE CORPORATION:
You have two cows.
You redesign them so they are one-tenth the size of an ordinary cow and produce twenty times the milk.
You then create a clever cow cartoon image called 'cowkimon' and market it worldwide.

A GERMAN CORPORATION:
You have two cows.
You re-engineer them so they live for 100 years, eat once a month, and milk themselves.

Financial and Political

AN ITALIAN CORPORATION:
You have two cows, but you don't know where they are.
You decide to have lunch.

A RUSSIAN CORPORATION:
You have two cows.
You count them and learn you have five cows. You count them again and learn you have 42 cows.
You count them again and learn you have 2 cows.
You stop counting cows and open another bottle of vodka.

A SWISS CORPORATION:
You have 5000 cows.
None of them belong to you. You charge the owners for storing them.

CHINESE CORPORATION:
You have two cows.
You have 300 people milking them. You claim that you have full employment, and high bovine productivity, and execute the newsman who reported the real situation.

AN INDIAN CORPORATION:
You have two cows.
You worship them.

Financial and Political

IRAQI CORPORATION:
Everyone thinks you have lots of cows. You tell them that you
have none.
No-one believes you, so they bomb the feck out of you and
invade your country.
You still have no cows, but at least now you are part of a
democracy.

AUSTRALIAN CORPORATION:
You have two cows.
Business seems pretty good. You close the office and go for a
few beers to celebrate.

WELSH CORPORATION:
You have two cows.
The one on the left looks very attractive.

A SCOTTISH CORPORATION:
You have two cows.
You put a fur coat on one and claim a new breed; you shove a
scaffolding tube up the behind of the other one, blow hard
and try to make music ... well sort of ...

AN ENGLISH CORPORATION:
You have two cows.
The Government says you have to buy a license to milk them,
but first you have to do a risk assessment, which only the
government is allowed to carry out. They charge you 5 times
the cost of doing it.
They find that the three-legged stool is a risk under health
and safety.

Financial and Political

You have to buy the EU approved 5 legged stool that is designed to support a milkmaid of up to 250 kilos. It is too heavy to carry.

The stool exceeds EU weight lifting limits for workers by 4 kilos, which just happens to be the weight of the fifth leg. To shift the stool from one cow to the other you therefore need a special EU approved trolley .

(To book and purchase training for accreditation to the stool moving trolley operatives charter please click here)

The new stool and trolley are so expensive that you have to mortgage one of the cows to pay for them and pay for the mandatory training course you must take to get your license to milk the cows.

You sell your milk to the supermarket chain that pays you peanuts for it, and then they sell it to their customers for four times what they paid you. Then they release a press statement about how wonderful they are to support British Cows.

The rest of the world thinks your cows are mad; but you, and your cows, know that it is not true, and anyway, the rest of the world have no intention of identifying and counting their mad cows; so people in other countries don't know their cows are really, really, barmy, do they?

You sell your cows to a Polish itinerant worker, and your farm to a Russian 'investment bank', and then you leave to buy a villa by the sea in a country where it is sunny and the cost of milk is a tenth the cost of milk at home.

They don't have a National Health Service ... but you are so happy and relaxed your health improves and you live to be a hundred!

Financial and Political

BENEFIT THIEVES ...

Financial and Political

A little boy goes to his dad and asks, 'What is Politics?'

Dad says, 'Well son, let me try to explain it this way:
I am the head of the family, so call me The Prime Minister.
Your mother is the administrator of the money, so we call her the Government. We are here to take care of your needs, so we will call you the People. The nanny, we will consider her the Working Class. And your baby brother, we will call him the Future. Now think about that and see if it makes sense.'

So the little boy goes off to bed thinking about what Dad has said. Later that night, he hears his baby brother crying, so he gets up to check on him.

He finds that the baby has severely soiled his nappy. So the little boy goes to his parents' room and finds his mother asleep. Not wanting to wake her, he goes to the nanny's room. Finding the door locked, he peeks in the keyhole and sees his father in bed with the nanny.

He gives up and goes back to bed.

The next morning, the little boy says to his father, 'Dad, I think I understand the concept of politics now.'

The father says, 'Good, son, tell me in your own words what you think politics is all about.'

The little boy replies, 'The Prime Minister is screwing the Working Class while the Government is sound asleep. The People are being ignored and the Future is in deep shit.'

Financial and Political

An Israeli doctor says 'Medicine in my country is so advanced that we can take a kidney out of one man put it in another and have him looking for work in six weeks'.

A German doctor says, 'That's nothing, we can take a lung out of one person put it in another and have him looking for work in four weeks.'

A Russian doctor says, 'In my country medicine is so advanced we can take half a heart out of one person put it in another and have them both looking for work in two weeks.'

The English doctor, not to be outdone, says, 'Hah! We can take two arseholes, stitch them together, put them in 10 Downing Street and have half the country looking for work within 24 hours'.

Official Announcement

Gordon Brown today announced that they are changing our Union Jack to a CONDOM because it more accurately reflects the government's political stance.
A Condom allows for inflation, halts production, destroys the next generation, protects a bunch of pricks and gives you a sense of security while you are actually being screwed.

It just cannot get more accurate than that.

Matters of Age

New Wine for Seniors

California vintners in the Napa Valley area, which primarily produce Pinot Blanc, Pinot Noir and Pinot Grigio wines, have developed a new hybrid grape that acts as an anti-diuretic.

It is expected to reduce the number of trips older people have to make to the bathroom during the night.
The new wine will be marketed as ...

PINO MORE

I HEARD IT THROUGH THE GRAPEVINE

Matters of Age

The question is: What Do Retired People Do All Day?

Working people frequently ask retired people what they do to make their days interesting.

Well, for example, the other day my wife and I went into town and went into a shop.

We were only in there for about 5 minutes. When we came out, there was a cop writing out a parking ticket.

We went up to him and said, 'Come on man, how about giving a senior citizen a break?'

He ignored us and continued writing the ticket. I called him a Nazi turd. He glared at me and started writing another ticket for having worn tyres.

So my wife called him a shit-head. He finished the second ticket and put it on the windshield with the first. Then he started writing a third ticket. This went on for about 20 minutes. The more we abused him, the more tickets he wrote.

Personally, we didn't care. We came into town by bus. We try to have a little fun each day now that we're retired. It's important at our age.

A BEAUTIFUL MESSAGE ABOUT GROWING OLD ...

Shit!.

I've forgotten it!

The Worst Age ...

'Sixty is the worst age to be,' said the 60-year-old man. 'You always feel like you have to pee and most of the time, you stand there and nothing comes out.'

'Ah, that's nothin,' said the 70-year-old. 'When you're seventy, you don't have a bowel movement anymore. You take laxatives, eat bran, and sit on the toilet all day and nothin' comes out!'

'Actually,' said the 80-year-old, 'Eighty is the worst age of all.'

'Do you have trouble peeing, too?' asked the 60-year old.

'No, I pee every morning at 6:00. I pee like a racehorse on a flat rock; no problem at all.'

'So do you have a problem with your bowel movement?'

'No, I have one every morning at 6:30.'

Exasperated, the 60-year-old said, 'You pee every morning at 6:00 and crap every morning at 6:30. So what's so bad about being 80?'

'I don't wake up until 7:00!'

Matters of Age

YOU KNOW YOU ARE LIVING IN 2013 when...

1 You accidentally enter your password on the microwave.

2 You haven't played solitaire with real cards in years.

3 You have a list of 15 phone numbers to reach your family of 3.

4 You e-mail the person who works at the desk next to you.

5 Your reason for not staying in touch with friends and family is that they don't have e-mail addresses.

6 You pull up in your own driveway and use your mobile phone to see if anyone is home to help you carry in the groceries.

7 Every commercial on television has a web site at the bottom of the screen.

8 Leaving the house without your mobile phone, which you didn't have the first 20 or 30 (or 60) years of your life, is now a cause for panic and you turn around to go and get it.

Matters of Age

10 You get up in the morning and go on line before getting your coffee.

11 You're reading this and nodding and laughing.

12 Even worse, you know exactly to whom you are going to forward this message.

13 You are too busy to notice there was no Number 9 on this list.

14 You actually scrolled back up to check that there wasn't a Number 9 on this list

AND NOW YOU ARE LAUGHING at yourself.

Go on, forward this to your friends.

You know you want to

Matters of Age

Getting older

As we age , we tend to end up seeing more of the medical establishment.

For example, my GP recommended me to a urologist who happened to be female.

I saw her yesterday and she is gorgeous. She's beautiful and unbelievably sexy.

She told me I have to stop masturbating. When I asked her why, she said, 'Because I'm trying to examine you ...'

Matters of Age

.New Alphabet For Senior Citizens

A is for apple, and **B** is for boat.
That used to be right, but now it won't float!
Age before beauty is what we once said,
But let's be a bit more realistic instead ...

A's for arthritis;

B's the bad back,

C's the chest pains, perhaps car-d-iac?

D is for dental decay and decline,

E is for eyesight, can't read that top line!

F is for fissures and fluid retention,

G is for gas which I'd rather not mention.

H ... high blood pressure—I'd rather it low;

I ... for incisions with scars you can show.

J is for joints, out of socket, won't mend,

K is for knees that crack when they bend.

L's for libido, what happened to sex?

Matters of Age

M is for memory, I forget what comes next.

N is neuralgia, in nerves way down low;

O is for osteo, bones that don't grow!

P for prescriptions, I have quite a few, just give me a pill and I'll be good as new!

Q is for queasy, is it fatal or flu?

R is for reflux, one meal turns to two.

S is for sleepless nights, counting my fears,

T is for Tinnitus; bells in my ears!

U is for urinary; troubles with flow;

V for vertigo, that's 'dizzy,' you know.

W for worry, NOW what's going 'round?

X is for X ray, and what might be found.

Y for another year I'm left here behind,

Z is for zest I still have – in my mind.

I've survived all the symptoms, my body's deployed, and I'm keeping twenty-six doctors fully employed!

Matters of Age

An elderly, white-haired man walked into a jewellery store one Friday evening with a beautiful young blonde at his side. He told the jeweller he was looking for a special ring for his girlfriend.

The jeweller looked through his stock and brought out a £5,000 ring. The old man said, 'No, I'd like to see something more special.'

At that statement, the jeweller went to his special stock and brought another ring over. 'Here's a stunning ring at only £40,000,' he said.

The young lady's eyes sparkled and her whole body trembled with excitement.

The old man seeing this said, 'We'll take it.'

The jeweller asked how payment would be made and the old man stated, 'By cheque. I know you need to make sure my cheque clears so I'll write it now, and you can call the bank on Monday morning to verify the funds and I'll pick the ring up on Monday afternoon,' he said.

On Monday morning, the jeweller phoned the old man and said 'Sir, there's no money in that account.'

'I know,' said the old man, 'but let me tell you about my weekend!'

All Seniors Aren't Senile.

AAADD
KNOW THE SYMPTOMS ... PLEASE READ!

Thank goodness there's a name for this disorder.
Somehow I feel better even though I have it!!
Recently, I was diagnosed with A.A.A.D.D.

Age Activated Attention Deficit Disorder.

This is how it manifests:
I decide to water my garden. As I turn on the hose in the
driveway, I look over at my car and decide it needs washing.

As I start toward the garage, I notice mail on the porch
table that I brought up from the mail box earlier.

I decide to go through the mail before I wash the car. I lay
my car keys on the table, put the junk mail in the garbage can
under the table, and notice that the can is full. So, I decide
to put the bills back on the table and take out the garbage
first.

But then I think, since I'm going to be near the mailbox when
I take out the garbage anyway, I may as well pay the bills
first.

I take my cheque book off the table, and see that there is
only one cheque left. My extra cheques are in my desk in the
study, so I go inside the house to my desk where I find the
can of Pepsi I'd been drinking.

Matters of Age

I'm going to look for my cheques, but first I need to push the Pepsi aside so that I don't accidentally knock it over.

The Pepsi is getting warm, and I decide to put it in the refrigerator to keep it cold. As I head toward the kitchen with the Pepsi, a vase of flowers on the counter catches my eye—they need water.

I put the Pepsi on the counter and discover my reading glasses that I've been searching for all morning. I decide I better put them back on my desk, but first I'm going to water the flowers.

I set the glasses back down on the counter, fill a container with water and suddenly spot the TV remote. Someone left it on the kitchen table. I realize that tonight when we go to watch TV, I'll be looking for the remote, but I won't remember that it's on the kitchen table, so I decide to put it back in the den where it belongs, but first I'll water the flowers.

I pour some water in the flowers, but quite a bit of it spills on the floor. So, I set the remote back on the table, get some towels and wipe up the spill. Then, I head down the hall trying to remember what I was planning to do.

At the end of the day the car isn't washed, the bills aren't paid, there is a warm can of Pepsi sitting on the counter, the flowers don't have enough water, there is still only 1 cheque in my cheque book, I can't find the remote, I can't find my glasses, and I don't remember what I did with the car keys.

Matters of Age

Then, when I try to figure out why nothing got done today, I'm really baffled because I know I was busy all damn day, ... and I'm really tired.

I realize this is a serious problem, and I'll try to get some help for it, but first I'll check my e-mail ...

Do me a favour. forward this message to everyone you know, because I don't remember who the hell I've sent it to.

Don't laugh – if this isn't you yet, your day is coming!!

Matters of Age

The couple were 85 years old and had been married for sixty years. Though they were far from rich, they managed to get by because they watched their pennies.

Though not young, they were both in very good health, largely due to the wife's insistence on healthy foods and exercise for the last decade.

One day, their good health didn't help when they went on a rare vacation and their plane crashed, sending them off to Heaven.

They reached the pearly gates, and St. Peter escorted them inside. He took them to a beautiful mansion, furnished in gold and fine silks, with a fully stocked kitchen and a waterfall in the master bath. A maid could be seen hanging their favourite clothes in the closet. They gasped in astonishment when he said, 'Welcome to Heaven. This will be your home now.'

The old man asked Peter how much all this was going to cost. 'Why, nothing,' Peter replied, 'remember, this is your reward in Heaven.'

The old man looked out the window and right there he saw a championship golf course, finer and more beautiful than any ever built on Earth. 'What are the greens fees?,' grumbled the old man.

Matters of Age

'This is heaven,' St. Peter replied. 'You can play for free, every day.'

Next they went to the clubhouse and saw the lavish buffet lunch, with every imaginable cuisine laid out before them, from seafood to steaks to exotic deserts, free flowing beverages.

'Don't even ask,' said St. Peter to the man. 'This is Heaven, it is all free for you to enjoy.'

The old man looked around and glanced nervously at his wife. 'Well, where are the low fat and low cholesterol foods and the decaffeinated tea?,' he asked.

That's the best part,' St. Peter replied. 'You can eat and drink as much as you like of whatever you like and you will never get fat or sick. This is Heaven!'

The old man pushed, 'No gym to work out at?'

'Not unless you want to,' was the answer.

'No testing my sugar or blood pressure or...'

'Never again. All you do here is enjoy yourself.'

The old man glared at his wife and said, 'You and your f**king bran Flakes. We could have been here ten years ago!'

I found **this** beautiful **winter** poem and **thought it** might be a comfort **to** you.

It was to me, and it's very well **written.**

ENJOY!

WINTER
a poem by Abigail Elizabeth McIntyre

F**k Me! It's Cold!

Matters of Age

Anyone under 50 - file for future review

Someone had to remind me, so I'm reminding you too. Don't laugh ... it is all true:

Perks of reaching 60 and heading towards 70!

1. Kidnappers are not very interested in you.

2. In a hostage situation you are likely to be released first.

3. No one expects you to run--anywhere.

4. People call at 9 pm and ask, did I wake you?

5. People no longer view you as a hypochondriac.

6. There is nothing left to learn the hard way.

7. Things you buy now won't wear out.

8. You can eat supper at 4 pm.

9. You can live without sex but not your glasses.

10. You get into heated arguments about pension plans.

11. You no longer think of speed limits as a challenge.

Matters of Age

12. You quit trying to hold your stomach in no matter who walks into the room.

13. You sing along with elevator music.

14. Your eyes won't get much worse.

15. Your investment in health insurance is finally beginning to pay off.

16. Your joints are more accurate meteorologists than the national weather service.

17. Your secrets are safe with your friends because they can't remember them either.

18. Your supply of brain cells is finally down to manageable size.

19. You can't remember who sent you this list.

And you notice these are all in Bold Print for your convenience.

Forward this to everyone you can remember right now!
And Never, under any circumstances, take a sleeping pill and a laxative on the same night.

So Cute!

INSTRUCTIONS FOR PROPERLY HUGGING A BABY:

1. First, uh, find a baby.

2. Second, be sure that the object you found was indeed a baby by employing classic sniffing techniques.

3. Next you will need to flatten the baby before actually beginning the hugging process.

So Cute!

4.   The 'paw slide' Simply slide paws around baby and prepare for possible close-up.

5.   Finally, if a camera is present, you will need to execute the difficult and patented 'hug, smile, and lean' so as to achieve the best photo quality.

If you don't pass this along, a dog will pee on your computer! I guess you didn't send it fast enough!

So Cute!

A CAT NAMED LUCKY ...

Are you expecting a heart wrenching story about a cat that got run over by a truck, lost a leg, dragged himself 100 kilometers after being bitten by a snake?

W R O N G!

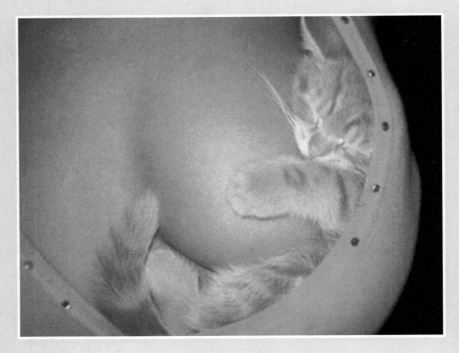

Information

Hi Folks ... take note:

FIRST MANY PEOPLE ARE UNAWARE OF

The main difference between http:// and https:// is
it's all about keeping you secure

HTTP stands for Hypertext Transport
a fancy way of saying it's a protocol (a language, in a manner
of speaking) for information to be passed back and forth
between web servers and clients.

The important thing is the letter S which makes the difference between HTTP and HTTPS.

The S (big surprise) stands for 'Secure'.

If you visit a website or webpage, and look at the address in
the web browser, it will likely begin with the
following:http://.

This means that the website is talking to your browser using
the regular 'unsecured language'. In other words, it is possible for someone to 'eavesdrop' on your computer's conversation with the website. If you fill out a form on the website,
someone might see the information you send to that site.

This is why you never ever enter your credit card number in
an http website!

Information

4 THINGS YOU PROBABLY NEVER KNEW ABOUT YOUR MOBILE PHONE

4 THINGS YOU PROBABLY NEVER KNEW YOUR
MOBILE PHONE COULD DO ...

There are a few things that can be done in times of grave
emergencies. Your mobile phone can actually be a life saver or
an emergency tool for survival ... Check out the things that
you can do with it:

FIRST Emergency

The Emergency Number worldwide for Mobile is 112. If you
find yourself out of the coverage area of your mobile; network and there is an emergency, dial 112 and the mobile will
search any existing network to establish the emergency number for you, and interestingly this number 112 can be dialed
even if the keypad is locked.

SECOND Have you locked your keys in the car?

Does your car have remote keyless entry? This may come in
handy someday. Good reason to own a cell phone: If you lock
your keys in the car and the spare keys are at home, call
someone at home on their mobile phone from your cell phone.
Hold your cell phone about a foot from your car door and
have the person at your home press the unlock button, holding it near the mobile phone on their end. Your car will unlock.
Saves someone from having to Drive your keys to you.

Information

Distance is no object. You could be hundreds of miles away, and if you can reach someone who has the other 'remote' for your car, you can unlock the doors (or the trunk).

Editor's Note: It works fine! We tried it out and it unlocked our car over a mobile phone!'

THIRD Hidden Battery Power

Imagine your mobile battery is very low. To activate, press the keys *3370# Your mobile will restart with this reserve and the instrument will show a 50% increase in battery. This reserve will get charged when you charge your mobile next time.

FOURTH How to disable a STOLEN mobile phone?

To check your Mobile phone's serial number, key in the following digits on your phone: * # 0 6 #
A 15 digit code will appear on the screen. This number is unique to your handset. Write it down and keep it somewhere safe. When your phone get stolen, you can phone your service provider and give them this code. They will then be able to block your handset so even if the thief changes the SIM card, your phone will be totally useless. You probably won't get your phone back, but at least you know that whoever stole it can't use/sell it either. If everybody does this, there would be no point in people stealing mobile phones.

Information

ATM – PIN Number Reversal – Good to Know

If you should ever be forced by a robber to withdraw money from an ATM machine, you can notify the police by entering your PIN # in reverse. For example, if your pin number is 1234, then you would put in 4321. The ATM system recognizes that your PIN number is backwards from the ATM card you placed in the machine. The machine will still give you the money you requested, but unknown to the robber, the police will be immediately dispatched to the location. This information was recently broadcast on CTV by Crime Stoppers however it is seldom used because people just don't know about it. Please pass this along to everyone.

This is the kind of information people don't mind receiving, so pass it on to your family and friends.

Information

A MOBILE IS A MOBILE WHEREEVER YOU LIVE-

I DIDN'T KNOW ABOUT 112 – DID YOU?

A bit of useful advice - verified by the Dorset Police .
The number does work from a mobile.

This actually happened to someone's daughter. Lauren was 19
yrs old and in college.

This story takes place over the Christmas/New Year's holiday break.

It was the Saturday before New Year and it was about
1.00pm in the afternoon, and Lauren was driving to visit a
friend, when an UNMARKED police car pulled up behind her
and put its lights on. Lauren's parents have 4 children (of
various ages) and have always told them never to pull over for
an unmarked car on the side of the road , but rather wait
until they get to a service station, etc

So Lauren remembered her parents' advice, and telephoned
112 from her mobile phone.

This connected her to the police dispatcher she told the dispatcher that there was an unmarked police car with a flashing blue light on his rooftop behind her and that she would
not pull over right away but wait until she was in a service
station or busy area.

The dispatcher checked to see if there was a police car

Information

where she was and there wasn't and he told her to keep driving, remain calm and that he had back-up already on the way.

Ten minutes later 4 police cars surrounded her and the unmarked car behind her.

One policeman went to her side and the others surrounded the car behind. They pulled the guy from the car and tackled him to the ground. The man was a convicted rapist and wanted for other crimes.

I never knew that bit of advice, but especially for a woman alone in a car, you do not have to pull over for an UNMARKED car.

Apparently police have to respect your right to keep going to a 'safe' place.

You obviously need to make some signals that you acknowledge them (i.e., put on your hazard lights) or call 112 like Lauren did.

Too bad the mobile phone companies don't give you this little bit of wonderful information.

So now it's your turn to let your friends know about 112 (112 is an emergency number on your mobile that takes you straight to the police because 999 does not work if you have no signal) .

This is good information that I did not know!
Please pass on to all your friends, especially any females.

Information

Aspirin

If you take an aspirin or a baby aspirin once a day, take it at night. The reason is aspirin has a 24-hour 'half-life'. Therefore, if most heart attacks happen in the wee hours of the morning, the aspirin would be strongest in your system.

FYI, aspirin lasts a really long time in your medicine chest ... years. When it gets old, it smells like vinegar.

WHY ASPIRIN BY YOUR BED save lives ... It is important to always have ASPIRIN in the home!

There are other symptoms of an heart attack besides the pain on the left arm. One must also be aware of an intense pain on the chin, as well as nausea and lots of sweating, however these symptoms may also occur less frequently.

NOTE: There may be no pain in the chest during an heart attack.

The majority of people (about 60%) who had an heart attack during their sleep, did not wake up. However, if it occurs, the chest pain may wake you up from your deep sleep. If that happens, IMMEDIATELY DISSOLVE TWO ASPIRINS IN YOUR MOUTH and swallow them with a bit of water.

Afterwards, phone a neighbor or a family member who lives very close by and state 'HEART ATTACK!' and that you have taken 2 ASPIRINS.

Information

Take a seat on a chair or sofa and wait for their arrival and DO NOT LIE DOWN!

A Cardiologist has stated that, if each person, after receiving this e-mail, sends it to 10 people, probably a life can be saved!

I have already shared the information! What about you? Forward this message ... IT MAY SAVE LIVES!

Brainteasers

Traffic Question

Most men will get this right!

Q: You are driving along a narrow two lane road with a NO PASSING FOR 2 MILES sign posted, and you come upon a bicycle rider. Do you:

(a)   Follow this slow-moving bicycle rider for the next 2 miles , or

(b)   Do you break the law and pass?

Which is the correct choice?

Scroll down ...

Brainteasers

A: Why take unnecessary risks and get a ticket?

Brainteasers

Name That Tune:

You'll kick yourself! ...

MOON RIVER
(Duh-h-h-h)

Hey, don't blame me ... I'm just forwarding this to those whose sense of humour I believe to be as warped as mine ... you were in that group.

Employment

Employee of the Month

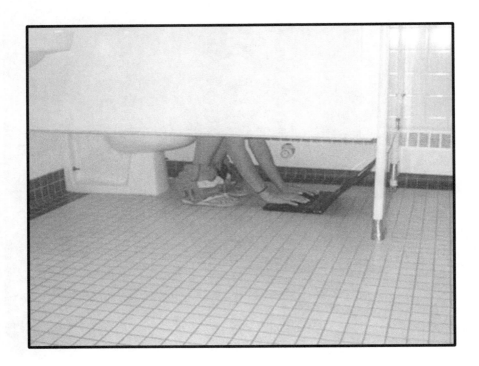

This is the level of dedication
we expect from all staff.
Keep up the good work!!

Employment

Elmo Factory

There is a factory in Northern Minnesota which makes the Tickle Me Elmo toys. The toy laughs when you tickle it under the arms.

Well, Carol is hired at The Tickle Me Elmo factory and she reports for her first day promptly at 8:00 am.

The next day at 8:45 am there is a knock at the Personnel Manager's door. The Foreman throws open the door and begins to rant about the new employee. He complains that she is incredibly slow and the whole line is backing up, putting the entire production line behind schedule.

The Personnel Manager decides he should see this for himself, so the two men march down to the factory floor. When they get there the line is so backed up that there are Tickle Me Elmo's all over the factory floor and they're really beginning to pile up.

At the end of the line stands Carol surrounded by mountains of Tickle Me Elmo's. She has a roll of plush Red fabric and a huge bag of small marbles.

Employment

The 2 men watch in amazement as she cuts a little piece of fabric, wraps it around two marbles and begins to carefully sew the little package between Elmo's legs.

The Personnel Manager bursts into laughter. After several minutes of hysterics he pulls himself together and approaches Carol.

'I'm sorry,' he says to her, barely able to keep a straight face, 'but I think you misunderstood the instructions I gave you yesterday ... your job is to give Elmo two test tickles."

If you don't send this to five friends right away, There will be five fewer people laughing in the world!

Employment

Dear Employees,

Due to the current financial situation caused by the slowdown of economy, Management has decided to implement a scheme to put workers of 40 years of age and above on early retirement. This scheme will be known as RAPE (Retire Aged People Early).

Persons selected to be RAPED can apply to management to be eligible for the SHAFT scheme (Special Help After Forced Termination). Persons who have been RAPED and SHAFTED will be reviewed under the SCREW programme (Scheme Covering Retired Early Workers). A person may be RAPED once, SHAFTED twice and SCREWED as many times as Management deems appropriate.

Only persons who have been RAPED can get AIDS (Additional Income for Dependants & Spouse) or HERPES (Half Earnings for Retired Personnel Early Severance).

Consequently persons who have AIDS or HERPES will not be SHAFTED or SCREWED any further by Management.

Persons who are not RAPED and are staying on will receive as much SHIT (Special High Intensity Training) as possible. Management has always prided itself on the amount of SHIT it gives employees. Should you feel that you do not receive enough SHIT, please bring this to the attention of your Supervisor.

They have been trained to give you all the SHIT you can handle.

Sincerely,
The Management

Employment

Does the manager/management know who you are?

Walking into the factory, the MD noticed a guy leaning against the wall, doing nothing.

He calmly said to the young man, 'How much do you earn?'

'I earn £2,000.00 a month, Sir. WHY?'

Without answering, the MD took out his wallet, and gave him £6,000.00 cash saying, 'Around here I pay people for working not standing and doing nothing! Here is 3 months salary, now get out and don't come back'

The young man disappeared.

Noticing onlookers, the MD said 'that applies to everybody in this company' He approached one of the onlookers and asked him 'who's the guy I just fired?'

The guy replied 'HE WAS THE PIZZA DELIVERY MAN SIR'

Women Only

Pregnancy, Oestrogen, and Women
PREGNANCY Q & A & more!

Q: Should I have a baby after 35?
A: No, 35 children is enough.

Q: I'm two months pregnant now. When will my baby move?
A: With any luck, right after he/she finishes college.

Q: What is the most reliable method to determine a baby's sex?
A: Childbirth.

Q: My wife is five months pregnant and so moody that sometimes she's borderline irrational.
A: So what's your question?

Q: My childbirth instructor says it's not pain I'll feel during labour, but pressure. Is she right?
A: Yes, in the same way that a tornado might be called an air current.

Q: When is the best time to get an epidural?
A: Right after you find out you're pregnant.

Q: Is there any reason I have to be in the delivery room while my wife is in labour?
A: Not unless the word 'divorce' means anything to you.

Women Only

Q: Is there anything I should avoid while recovering from childbirth?
A: Yes, pregnancy.

Q: Our baby was born last week. When will my wife begin to feel and act normal again?
A: When the kids are in college.

'OESTROGEN ISSUES'

10 WAYS TO KNOW IF YOU HAVE 'OESTRO-GEN ISSUES'

1. Everyone around you has an attitude problem.

2. You're adding chocolate chips to your cheese omelet.

3. The dryer has shrunk every last pair of your jeans.

4. Your husband is suddenly agreeing to everything you say.

5. You 're using your mobile phone to dial up every bumper sticker that says: 'How's my driving-call 1- 800-

6. Everyone's head looks like an invitation to batting practice.

7. Everyone seems to have just landed here from 'outer space.'

Women Only

9. You're sure that everyone is scheming to drive you crazy.

10. The ibuprofen bottle is empty and you bought it yester-day.

TOP TEN THINGS ONLY WOMEN UNDERSTAND

10. Cats' facial expressions.

9. The need for the same style of shoes in different colours.

8. Why bean sprouts aren't just weeds.

7. Fat clothes.

6. Taking a car trip without trying to beat your best time.

5. The difference between beige, ecru, cream, off-white, and eggshell.

4. Cutting your hair to make it grow.

3. Eyelash curlers.

2. The inaccuracy of every bathroom scale ever made.

AND, the Number One thing only women understand:
OTHER WOMEN

Women Only

Why I'm worn out

I'm tired

Yes, I'm tired. For several years I've been blaming it on middle age, poor blood, lack of vitamins, air pollution, Saccharin, obesity, dieting, yellow wax build up and another dozen maladies that make you wonder if life is really worth living.

But I found out that it isn't any of those.

I'm tired because I'm overworked.

The population of this country is 51 million.

21 million of those are retired.
That leaves 30 million to do the work.

There are 19 million at school.
That leaves 11 million to do the work.

2 million are unemployed and 4 million are employed by the Government to look after us.
That leaves 5 million to do the work.

Women Only

1 million are in the armed forces, which leaves 4 million to do the work.

3 million are employed by County & Borough Councils to help the Government to look after us.
That leaves 1 million to do the work.
There are 620,000 people in hospital and 379,998 in prisons.
Which leaves two people to do the work.

YOU & ME

And you're sitting on your arse reading this.
No wonder I'm bloody tired!

Women Only

A WOMAN'S WEEK AT THE GYM

If you read this without laughing out   there is something
wrong with you. This is dedicated to   who ever
attempted to get into a regular workout routine.

Dear Diary,
For my birthday this year, my Husband (the dear) purchased
a week of personal training at the local health club for me.

Although I am still in great shape since being a high school
football cheerleader 43 years ago, I decided it would be a
good idea to go ahead and give it a try.

I called the club and made my reservations with a personal
trainer named Christo, who identified himself as a 26-year-
old aerobics instructor and model for athletic clothing and
swim wear.

My husband seemed pleased with my enthusiasm to get started! The club encouraged me to keep a diary to chart my
progress.

MONDAY:
Started my day at 6:00 a.m. Tough to get out of bed, but
found it was well worth it when I arrived at the health club
to find Christo waiting for me. He is something of a Greek
god - with blond hair, dancing eyes and a dazzling white smile.
Woo Hoo!!

Women Only

Christo gave me a tour and showed me the machines. I enjoyed watching the skillful way in which he conducted his aerobics class after my workout today. Very inspiring!

Christo was encouraging as I did my sit-ups, although my gut was already aching from holding it in the whole time he was around. This is going to be a FANTASTIC week-!!

TUESDAY:
I drank a whole pot of coffee, but I finally made it out the door. Christo made me lie on my back and push a heavy iron bar into the air then he put weights on it! My legs were a little wobbly on the treadmill, but I made the full mile. His rewarding smile made it all worthwhile. I feel GREAT-!! It's a whole new life for me.

WEDNESDAY:
The only way I can brush my teeth is by laying the toothbrush on the counter and moving my mouth back and forth over it. I believe I have a hernia in both pectorals. Driving was OK as long as I didn't try to steer or stop. I parked on top of a GEO in the club parking lot.

Christo was impatient with me, insisting that my screams bothered other club members. His voice is a little too perky for that early in the morning and when he scolds, he gets this nasally whine that is VERY annoying.

Women Only

My chest hurt when I got on the so Christo put me
on the stair monster. Why the hell anyone invent a
machine to simulate an activity obsolete by eleva-
tors? Christo told me it would help me get in shape and enjoy
life. He said some other shit too.

THURSDAY:
Asshole was waiting for me with his vampire-like teeth
exposed as his thin, cruel lips were pulled back in a full snarl.
I couldn't help being a half an hour late - it took me that long
to tie my shoes.

He took me to work out with dumbbells. When he was not
looking, I ran and hid in the restroom. He sent some skinny
bitch to find me.

Then, as punishment, he put me on the rowing machine —
which I sank.

FRIDAY:
I hate that bastard Christo more than any human being has
ever hated any other human being in the history of the world.
Stupid, skinny, anemic, anorexic little aerobic instructor. If
there was a part of my body I could move without unbearable
pain, I would beat him with it.

Christo wanted me to work on my triceps. I don't have any
triceps! And if you don't want dents in the floor, don't hand
me the damn barbells or anything that weighs more than a
sandwich.

Women Only

The treadmill flung me off and I landed on a health and nutrition teacher. Why couldn't it have been someone softer, like the drama coach or the choir director?

SATURDAY:
Satan left a message on my answering machine in his grating, shrilly voice wondering why I did not show up today. Just hearing his voice made me want to smash the machine with my planner; however, I lacked the strength to even use the TV remote and ended up catching eleven straight hours of the Weather Channel.

SUNDAY:
I'm having the Church van pick me up for services today so I can go and thank GOD that this week is over. I will also pray that next year my husband will choose a gift for me that is fun — like a root canal or a hysterectomy. I still say if God had wanted me to bend over, he would have sprinkled the floor with diamonds!!!

Send this to a friend who needs to laugh. We all need a good laugh

And Finally ...

A photo like this just doesn't come along every day!

One of the reasons Mummy

wont let him be king!

And Finally ...

This is an Incredible story!

In 1986, Peter Davies was on holiday in Kenya after graduating from Northwestern University.

On a hike through the bush, he came across a young bull elephant standing with one leg raised in the air. The elephant seemed distressed, so Peter approached it very carefully.

He got down on one knee, inspected the elephant's foot, and found a large piece of wood deeply embedded in it. As carefully and as gently as he could, Peter worked the wood out with his knife, after which the elephant gingerly put down its foot.

The elephant turned to face the man, and with a rather curious look on its face, stared at him for several tense moments

Peter stood frozen, thinking of nothing else but being trampled. Eventually the elephant trumpeted loudly, turned, and walked away.

Peter never forgot that elephant or the events of that day.

Twenty years later, Peter was walking through the Chicago Zoo with his teenaged son.

As they approached the elephant enclosure, one of the creatures turned and walked over to near where Peter and his son Cameron were standing. The large bull elephant stared at Peter, lifted its front foot off the ground, then put it down.

And Finally ...

The elephant did that several times then trumpeted loudly, all the while staring at the man.

Remembering the encounter in 1986, Peter could not help wondering if this was the same elephant.

Peter summoned up his courage, climbed over the railing, and made his way into the enclosure.

He walked right up to the elephant and stared back in wonder

The elephant trumpeted again, wrapped its trunk around one of Peter legs and slammed him against the railing, killing him instantly.

Probably wasn't the same elephant.

This is for everyone who sends me those heart-warming bull-shit stories.

And Finally ...

London Times Obituary of the late Mr. Common Sense

Interesting and sadly rather true.

'Today we mourn the passing of a beloved old friend, Common Sense, who has been with us for many years. No one knows for sure how old he was, since his birth records were long ago lost in bureaucratic red tape. He will be remembered as having cultivated such valuable lessons as: Knowing when to come in out of the rain; why the early bird gets the worm; Life isn't always fair; and maybe it was my fault.

Common Sense lived by simple, sound financial policies (don't spend more than you can earn) and reliable strategies (adults, not children, are in charge).

His health began to deteriorate rapidly when well-intentioned but overbearing regulations were set in place. Reports of a 6-year-old boy charged with sexual harassment for kissing a classmate; teens suspended from school for using mouthwash after lunch; and a teacher fired for reprimanding an unruly student, only worsened his condition.

Common Sense lost ground when parents attacked teachers for doing the job that they themselves had failed to do in disciplining their unruly children.

It declined even further when schools were required to get parental consent to administer sun lotion or an Aspirin to a

And Finally ...

student; but could not inform parents when a student became pregnant and wanted to have an abortion.

Common Sense lost the will to live as the churches became businesses; and criminals received better treatment than their victims.

Common Sense took a beating when you couldn't defend yourself from a burglar in your own home and the burglar could sue you for assault.

Common Sense finally gave up the will to live, after a woman failed to realize that a steaming cup of coffee was hot. She spilled a little in her lap, and was promptly awarded a huge settlement.

Common Sense was preceded in death by his parents, Truth and Trust; his wife, Discretion; his daughter, Responsibility; and his son, Reason. He is survived by his 4 stepbrothers; I Know My Rights, I Want It Now, Someone Else Is To Blame, and I'm A Victim.

Not many attended his funeral because so few realized he was gone. If you still remember him, pass this on. If not, join the majority and do nothing

And Finally ...

THE YEAR'S BEST [actual] HEADLINES:

crack found on
governor's daughter
[Imagine that!]

Something Went Wrong
in Jet Crash, Expert Says
[No, really?]

Police Begin Campaign to Run
Down Jaywalkers
[Now that's taking things a bit far!]

is there a ring of debris
around uranus?
[Not if I wipe thoroughly!]

And Finally ...

Panda Mating Fails; Veterinarian Takes Over
[What a guy!]

Miners Refuse to Work after Death
[No-good-for-nothing' lazy so-and-sos!]

Juvenile Court to Try Shooting Defendant
[See if that works any better than a fair trial!]

War Dims Hope for Peace
[I can see where it might have that effect!]

if strike isn't settled quickly, it may last a while
[You think?]

And Finally ...

cold wave linked to temperatures
[Who would have thought!]

Enfield (London) Couple Slain;
Police Suspect Homicide
[They may be on to something!]

Red Tape Holds Up New Bridges
[You mean there's something stronger than duct tape?]

man struck by lightning: faces battery charge
[he probably IS the battery charge!]

And Finally ...

New Study of Obesity Looks for Larger Test Group
[Weren't they fat enough?!]

astronaut takes blame for gas in spacecraft
[That's what he gets for eating those beans!]

Kids Make Nutritious Snacks
[Taste like chicken?]

Local High School Dropouts Cut in Half
[Chainsaw Massacre all over again!]

Hospitals are Sued by 7 Foot Doctors
[Boy, are they tall!]

And Finally ...

And the winner is ...

Typhoon Rips Through Cemetery; Hundreds Dead

And Finally ...

I'm **Still waiting ...**

I did what you told me.

I sent the email to 10 people like you said.

I'm still waiting for that miracle to happen.

To all my friends who in the last year sent me best 'wishes', chain letters, 'angel' letters or other promises of good luck if I forwarded something,

NONE OF THAT CRAP WORKED!

For 2013, could you please just send money, Vodka, chocolate, movie tickets or PETROL VOUCHERS!!

Thank you!

And Finally ...

THIS IS AMAZING !

FORWARD THIS MESSAGE ON TO FIVE PEOPLE

and

within   3 minutes.....

FUCK ALL

WILL HAPPEN!!!!!

I TRIED IT **TWICE** AND IT WORKED
BOTH TIMES

ABSOLUTELY FUCK ALL HAPPENED !!!

THIS REALLY WORKS

PASS THIS ON - MORE PEOPLE NEED TO KNOW

Dear Friends

With a New Year now upon us, I'd like to extend my heart-felt appreciation to all of you who have taken the time and trouble to send me 'forwards' over the past 12 months. Thank you for making me feel safe, secure, blessed and healthy.

Extra thanks to whoever sent me the email about rat crap in the glue on envelopes - because I now have to go get a wet towel every time I need to seal an envelope.

Also, I scrub the top of every can I open for the same reason.

Because of your genuine concern, I no longer drink Coca Cola because I know it can remove toilet stains, which is not exactly an appealing characteristic.

I no longer check the coin return on pay phones because I could be pricked with a needle infected with AIDS.

I no longer use cancer-causing deodorants even though I smell like a water buffalo on a hot day.

I no longer go to shopping centres because someone might drug me with a cologne sample and rob me.

I no longer eat KFC because their 'chickens' are actually horrible mutant freaks with no eyes or feathers.

I no longer worry about my soul because at last count, I have 363,214 Angels looking out for me.

Thanks to you, I have learned that God only answers my prayers if I forward an e-mail to seven of my friends and make a wish within five minutes.

I no longer have any savings because I gave it to a sick girl on the Internet who is about to die in the hospital (for the 1,387,258th time).

I no longer have any money at all in fact - but that will change once I receive the £15,000 that Microsoft and AOL are sending me for participating in their special on-line email program.

Yes, I want to thank you all so much for looking out for me that I will now return the favour!

If you don't send this e-mail to at least 144,000 people in the next 7 minutes, a large pigeon with a wicked case of diaorreah will land on your head at 5:00PM GMT this afternoon. I know this will occur because it actually happened to a friend of my next door neighbour's ex-mother-in-law's second husband's cousin's beautician!

Have a great new Year All!

With warm wishes

Stuart

CPSIA information can be obtained at www.ICGtesting.com
Printed in the USA
LVOW011114060613

3549LVUK00009B/20/P